AF290931

CHARLES AND SAATCHI
THE DOGS

JEAN PIGOZZI

FOREWORD BY CHARLES SAATCHI

DAMIANI

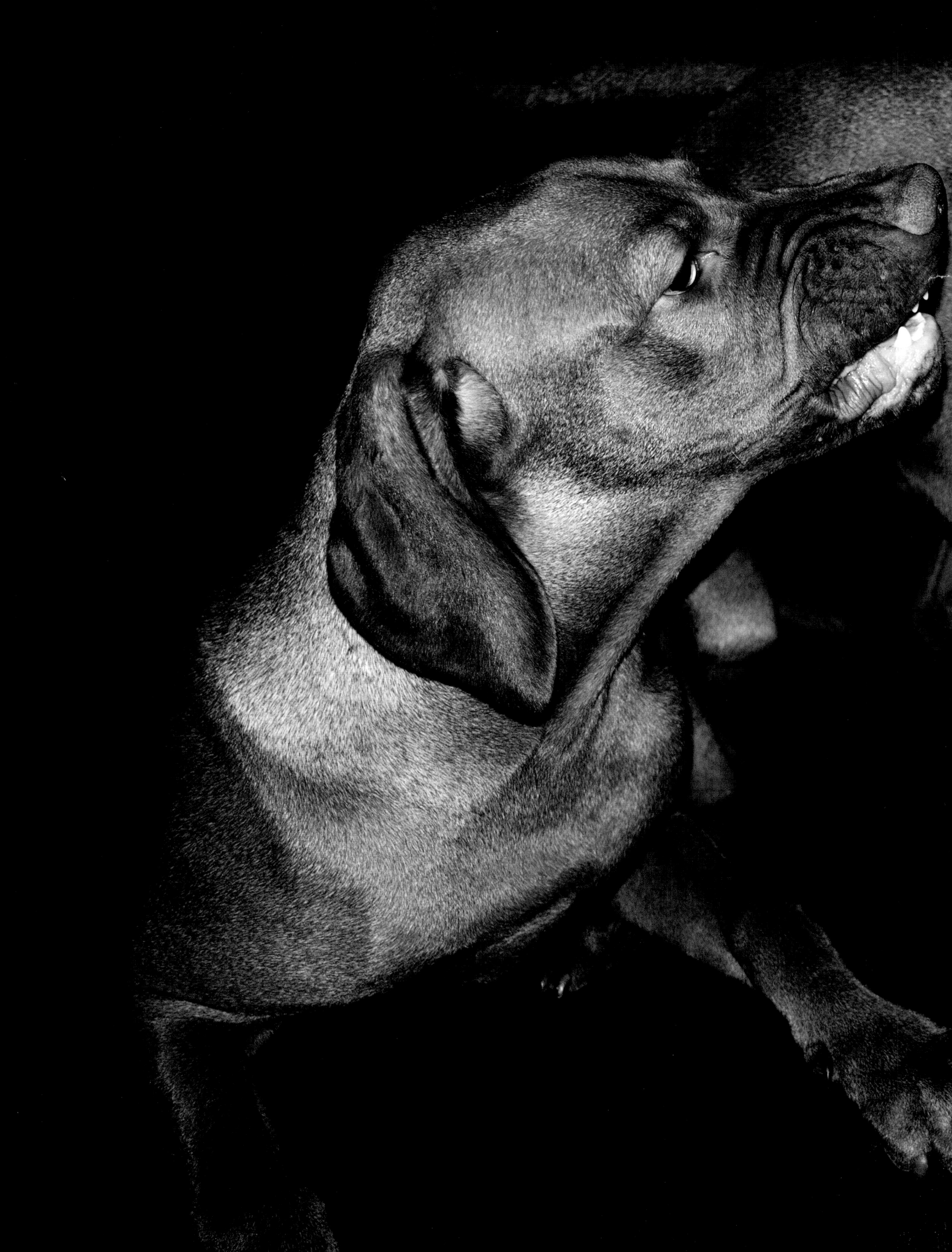

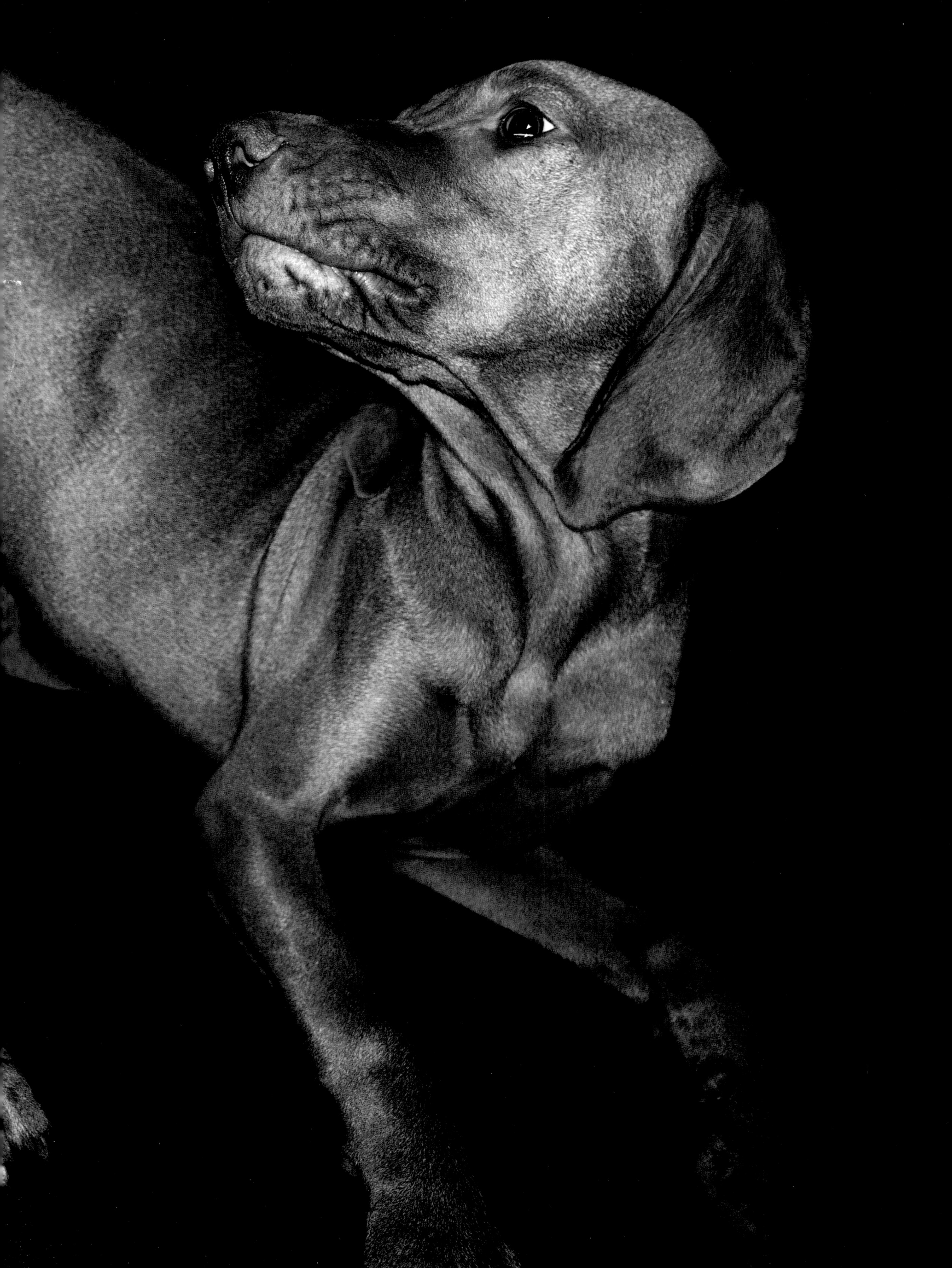

MY LIFE AS A DOG

Do you believe in reincarnation?

According to a Gallup Poll, about a quarter of us in the West firmly do.

The figure is even higher among hundreds of

millions of Hindus and Buddhists,

who adhere to the notion of an immortal soul.

They are convinced that we return again and again to life on Earth,

in one form or another—a cat, a mouse, an elephant, a bird—

before once again assuming human form.

Personally, I have always sensed that the Fates intend

to resurrect me for my next life as a dog.

And what could be more agreeable than enjoying my future days as one of Jean Pigozzi's pets?

As you can see here, they are particularly handsome creatures,

and that is clearly befitting. Also appropriately, you will also note they are

keenly intelligent, and highly sophisticated.

With Mr. Pigozzi as their owner, their important daily activities are being

recorded for posterity by one of the world's great photographers.

His remarkable skills in observational studies are as outstanding as

Cindy Sherman's mastery of self-portraiture.

With good fortune, when my time comes, I will spring back to life

as an offspring of one of the noble dogs pictured here,

and enjoy many serene years as one of

Mr. Pigozzi's most treasured companions.

—*CHARLES SAATCHI, London, September 2017*

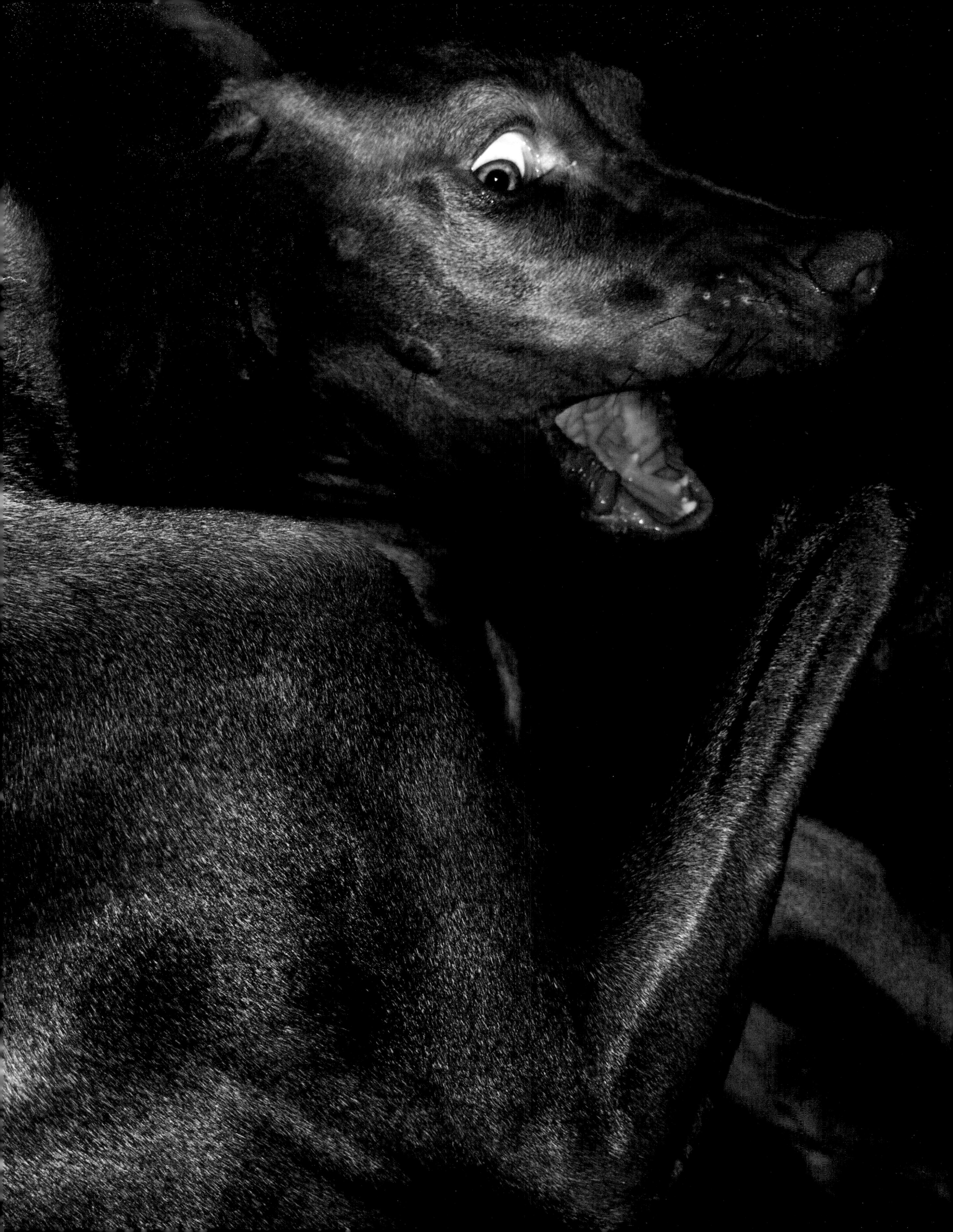

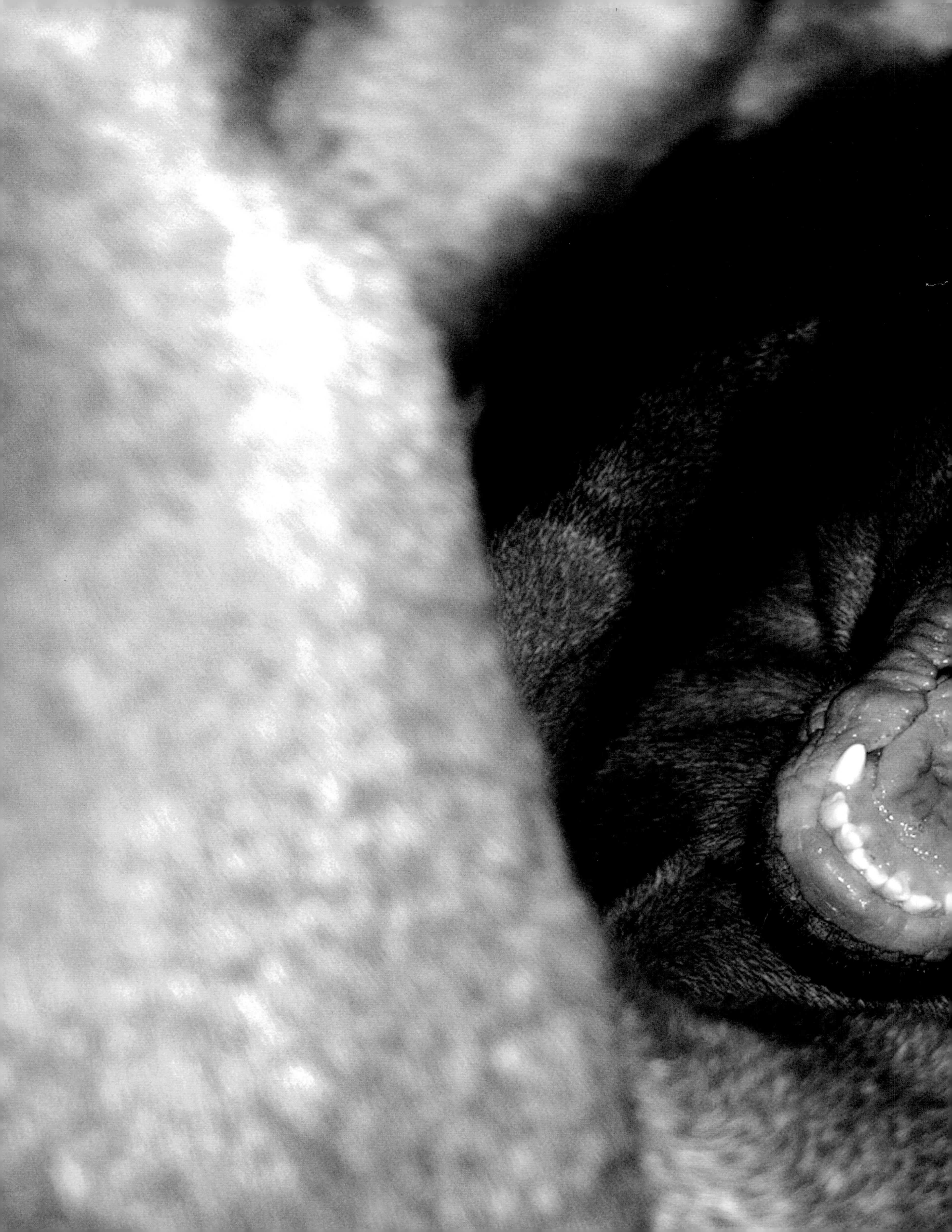

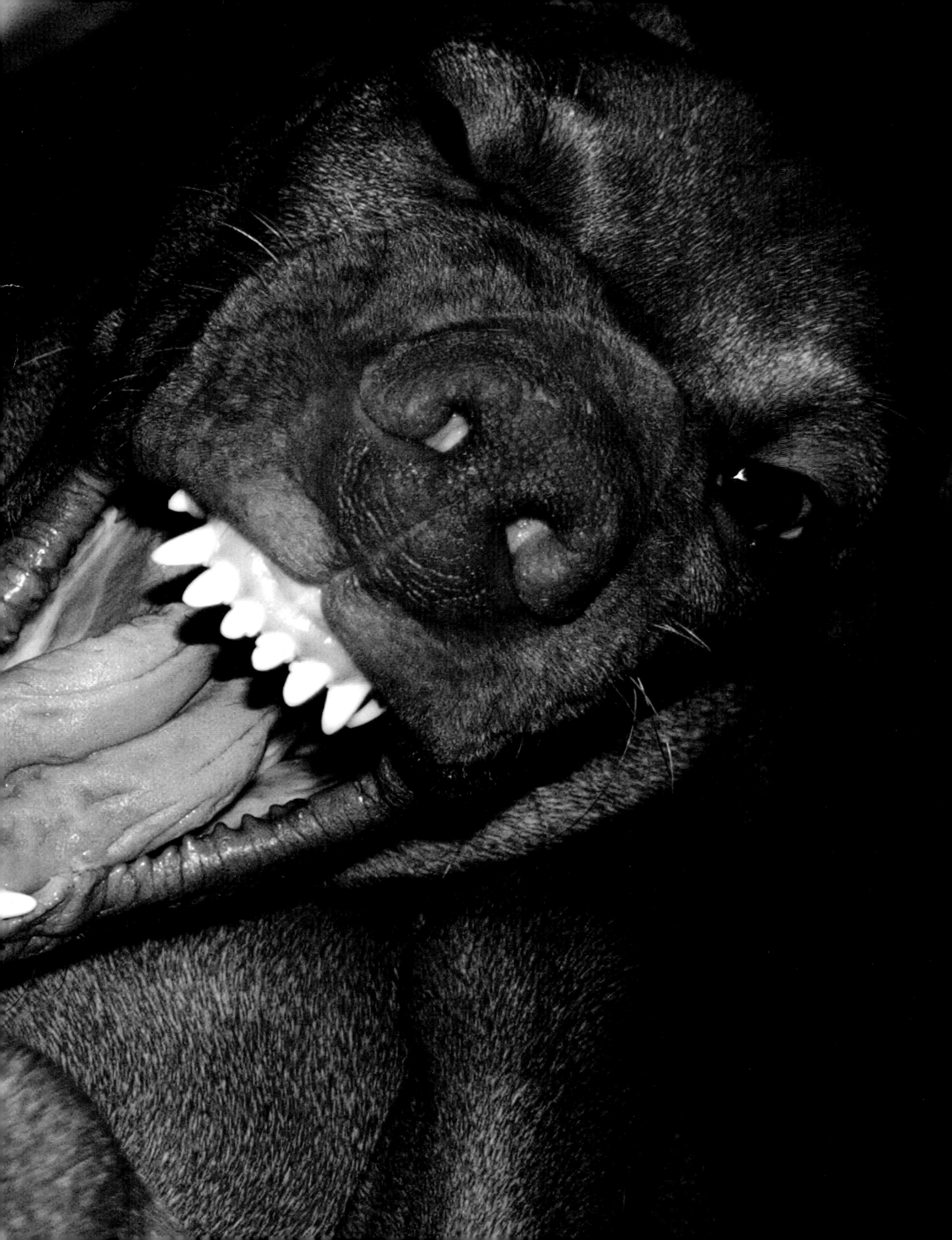

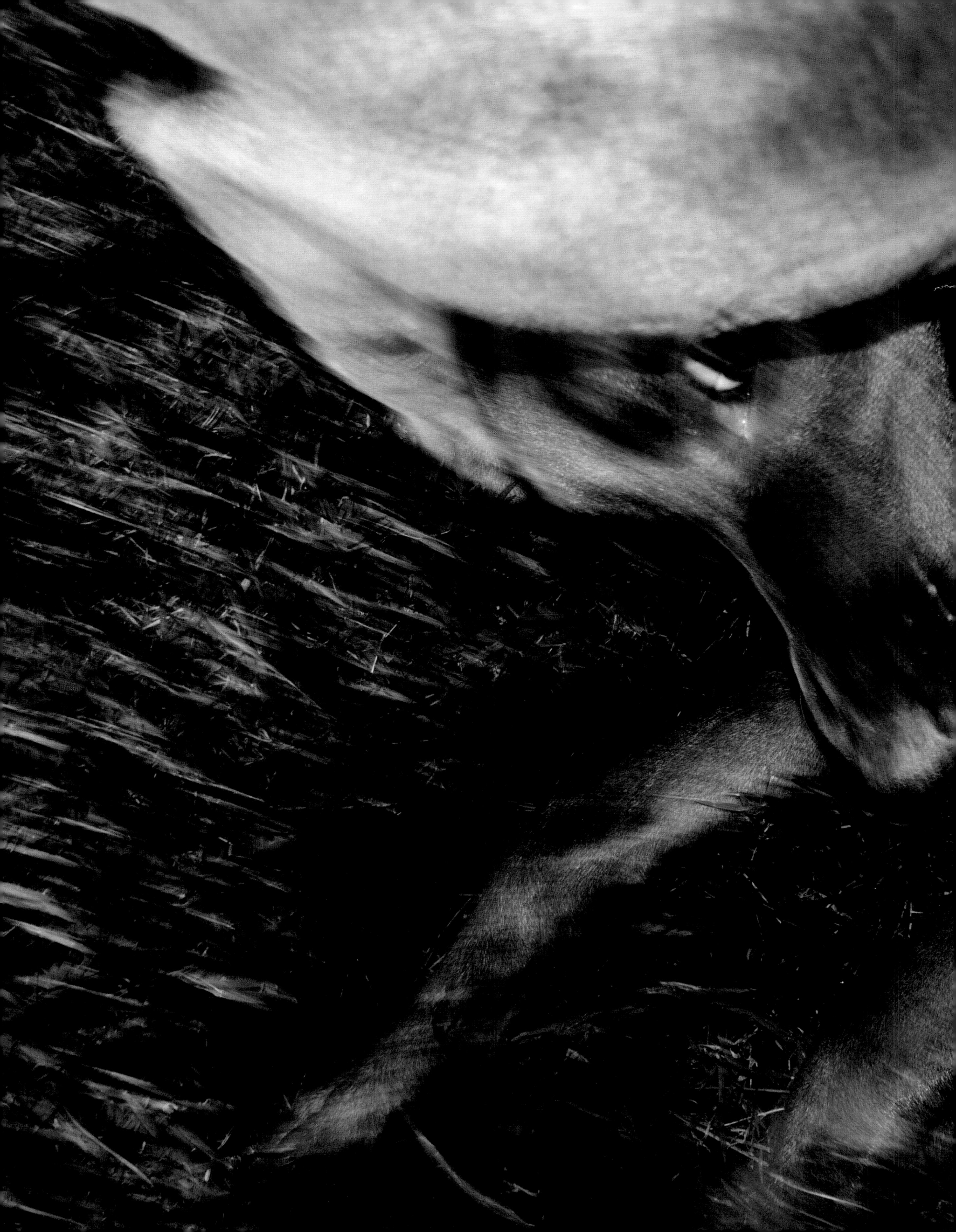

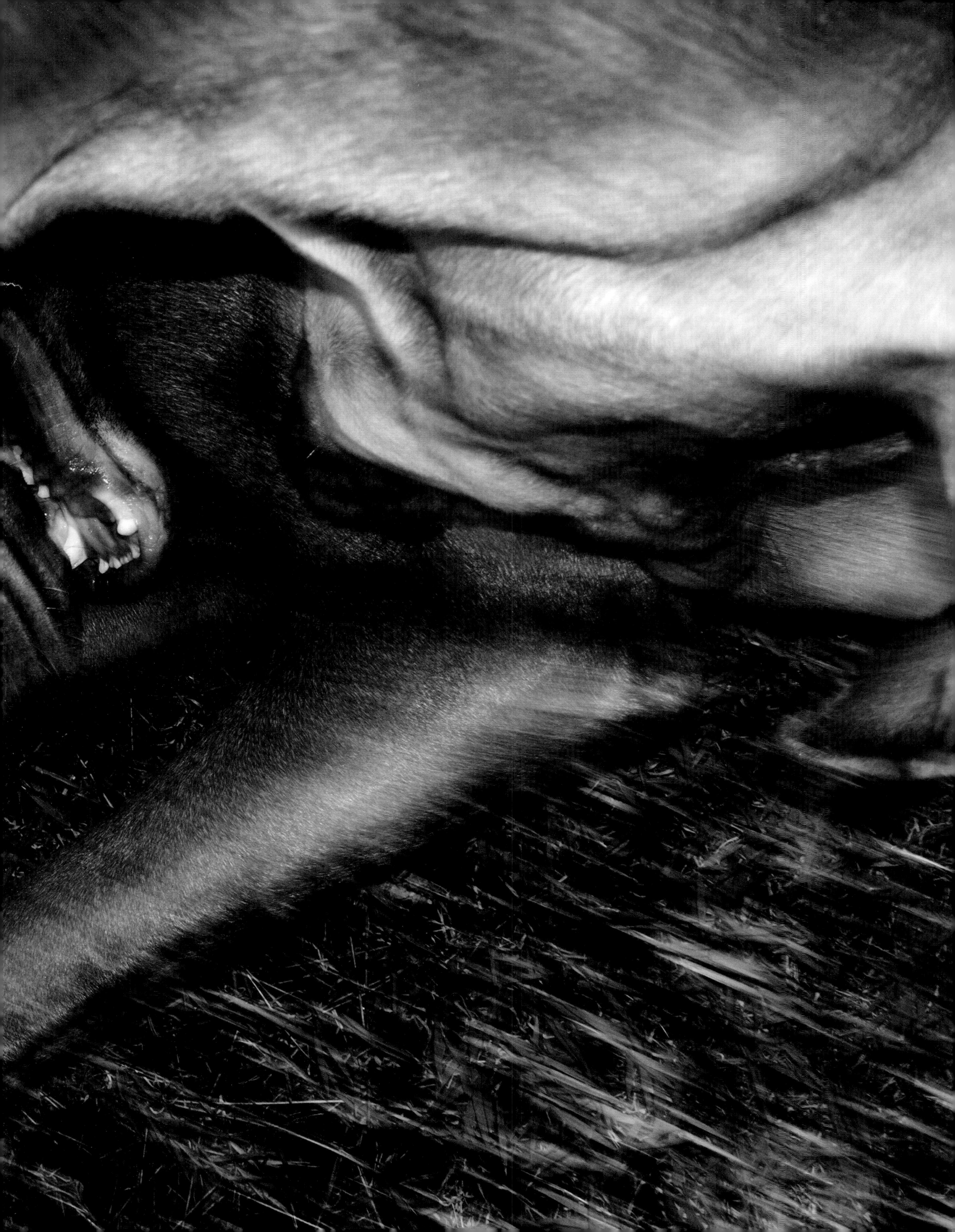

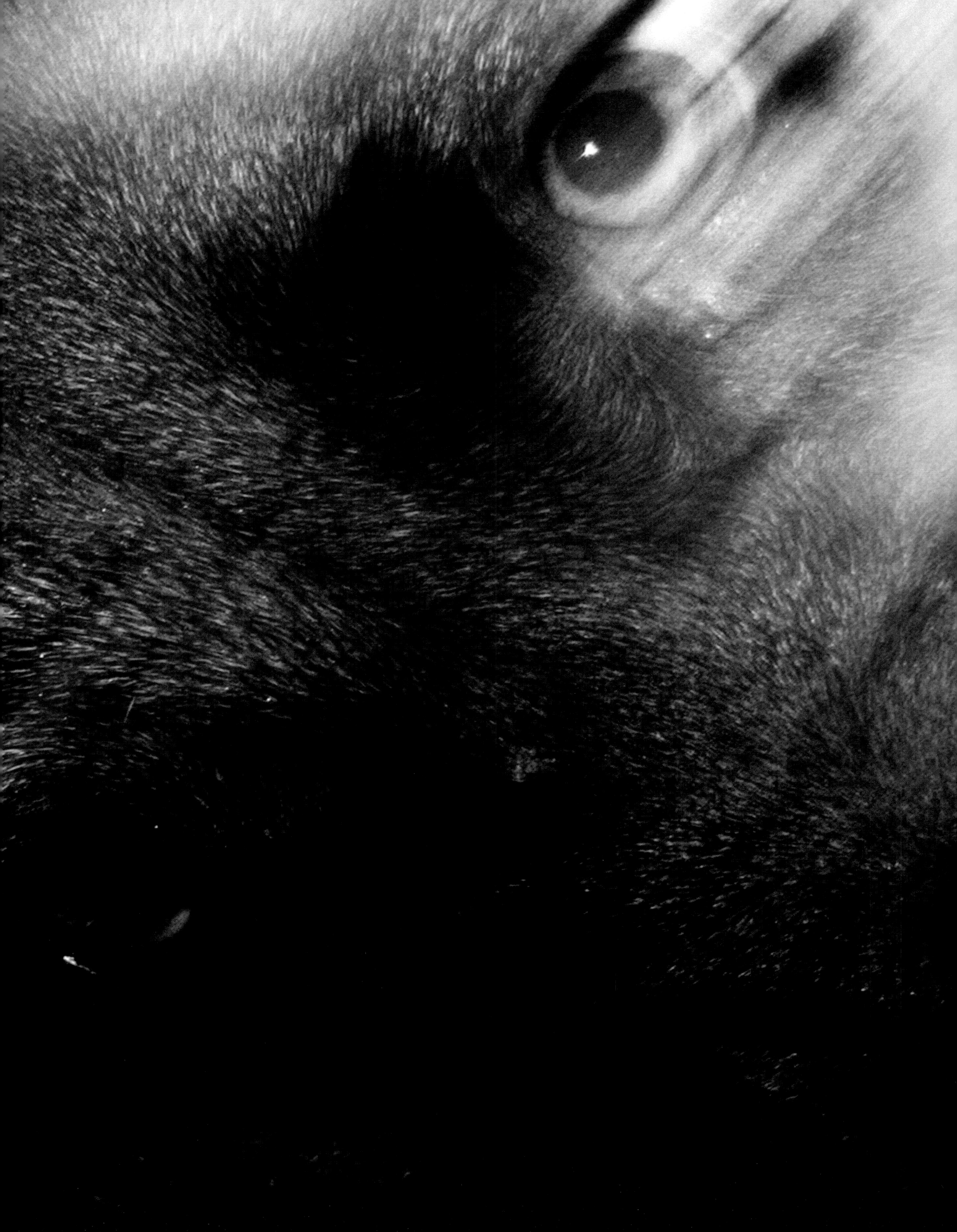

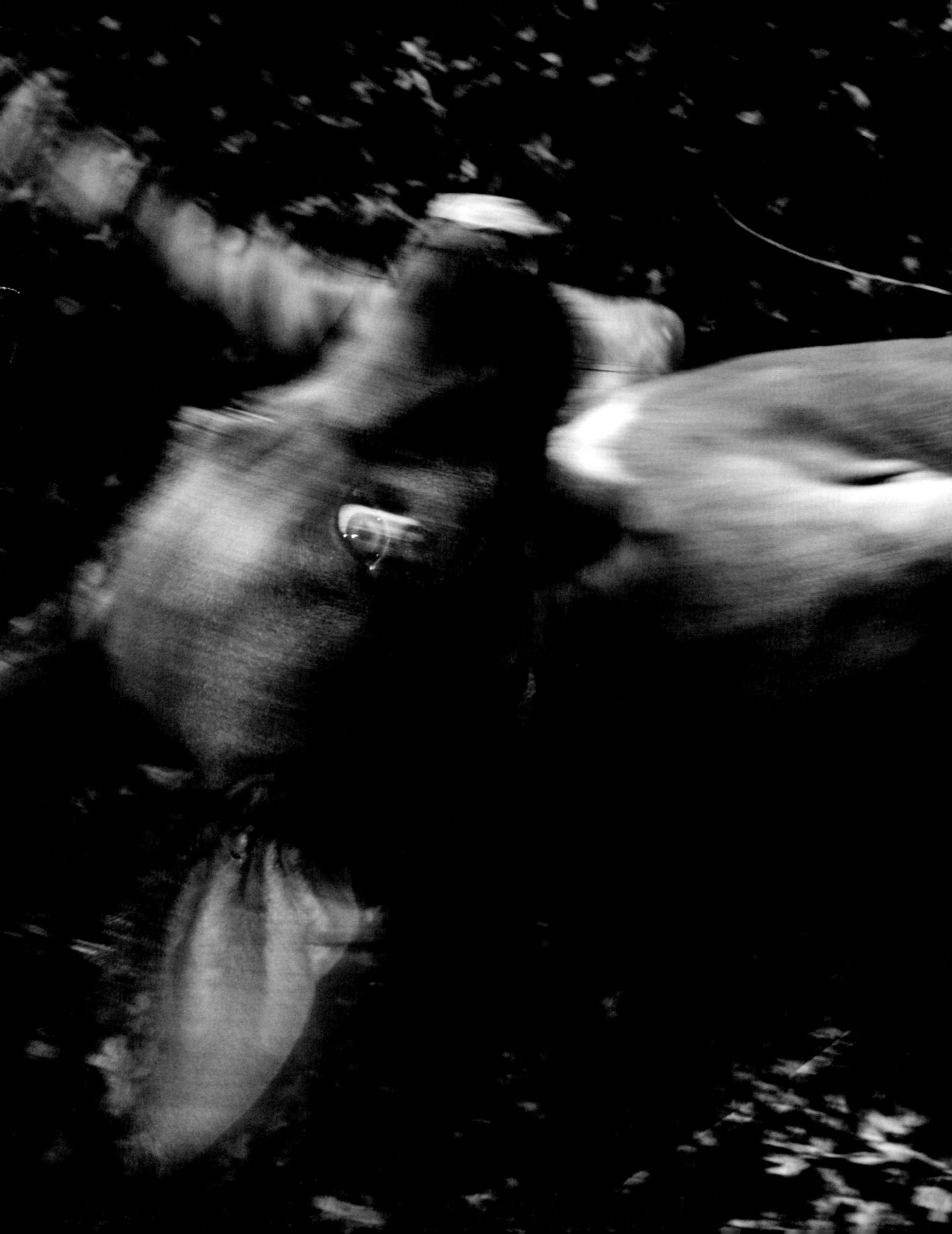

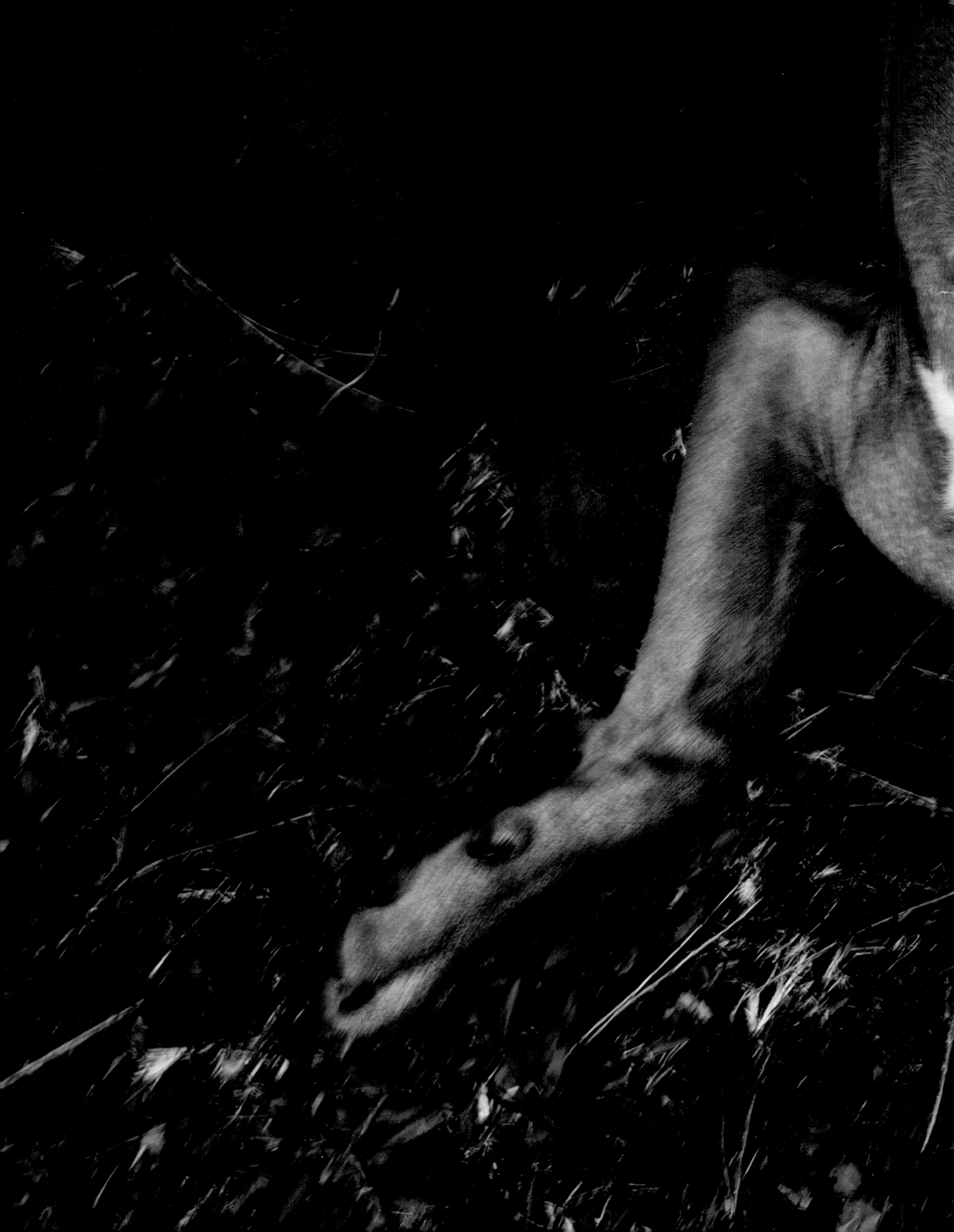

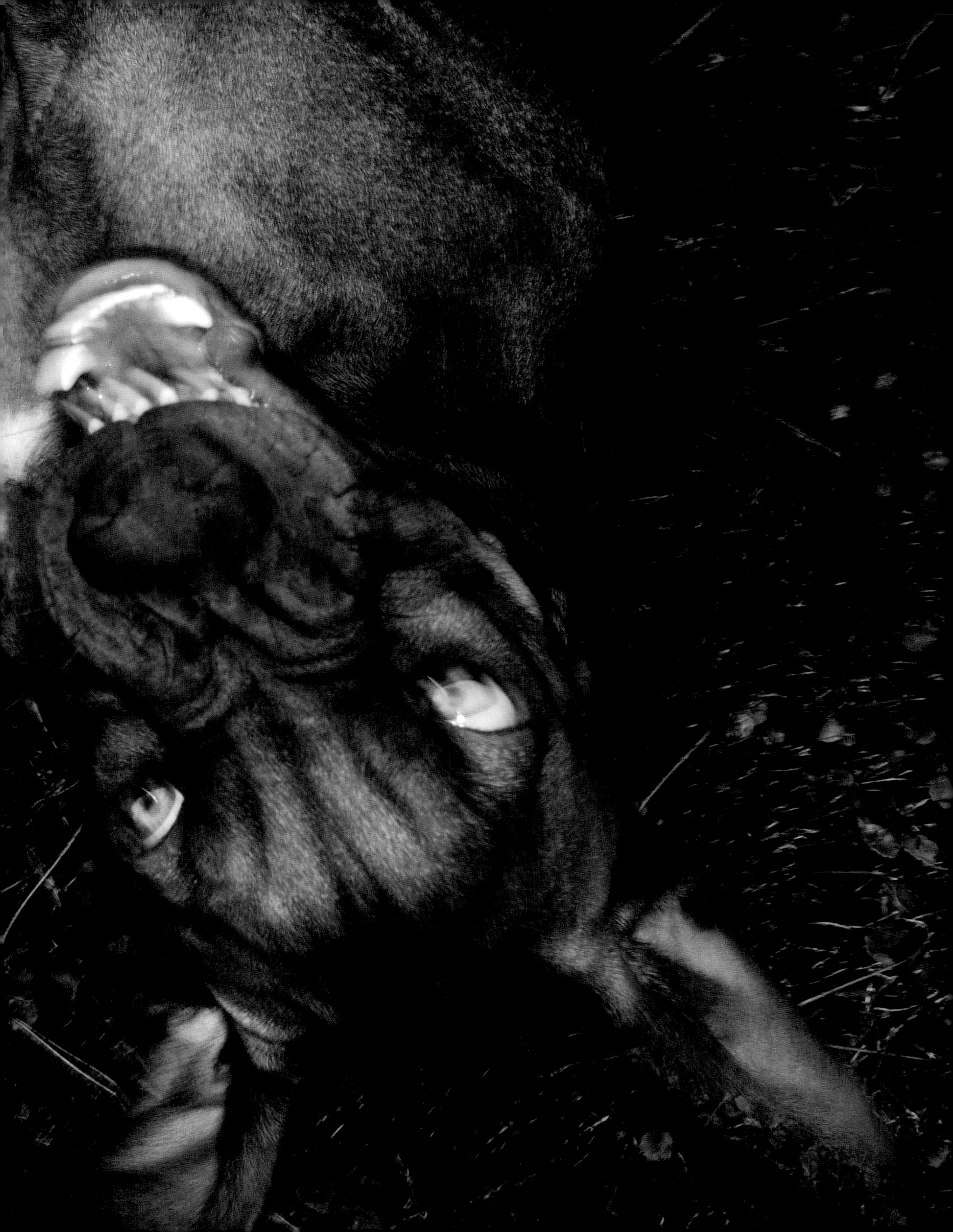

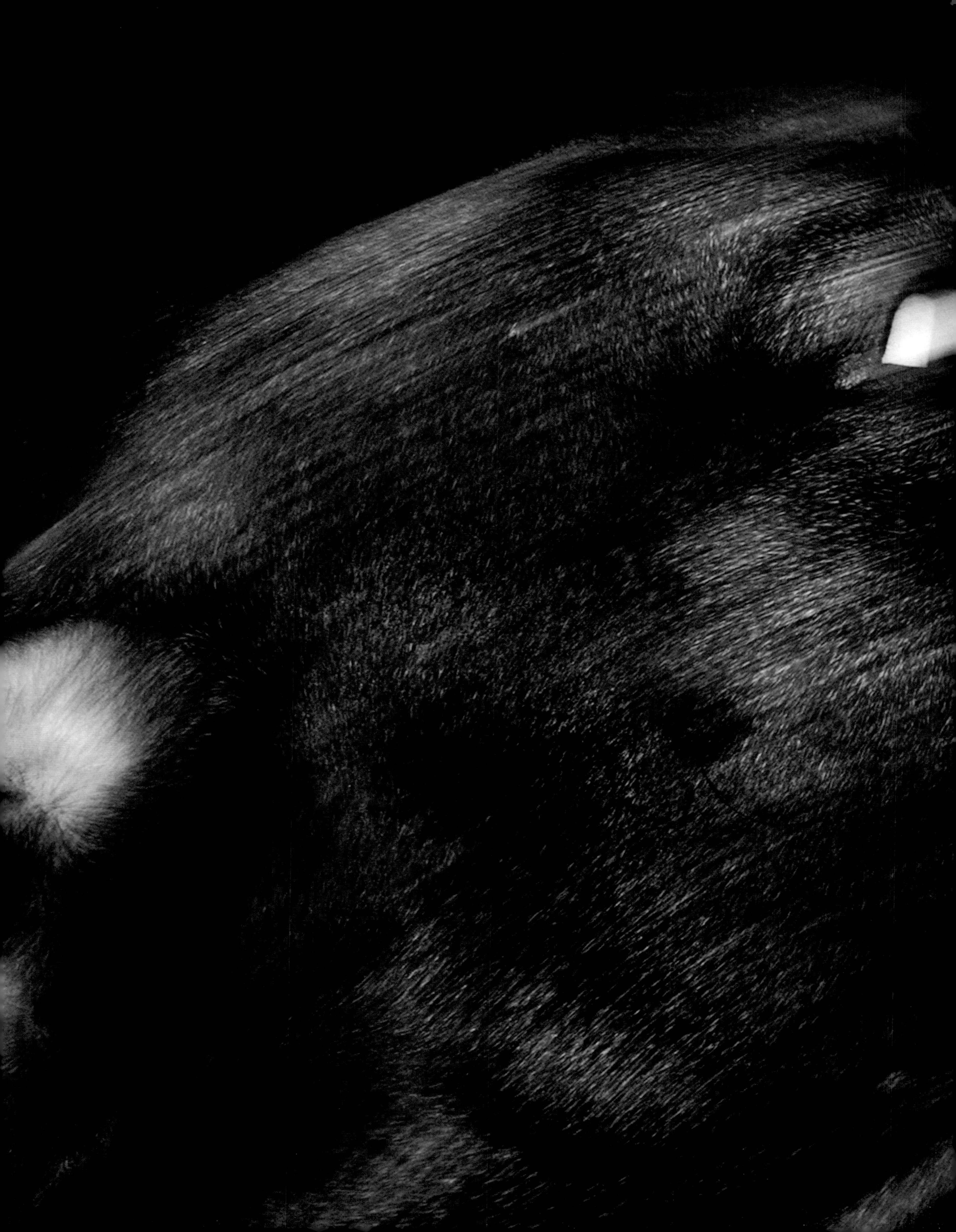

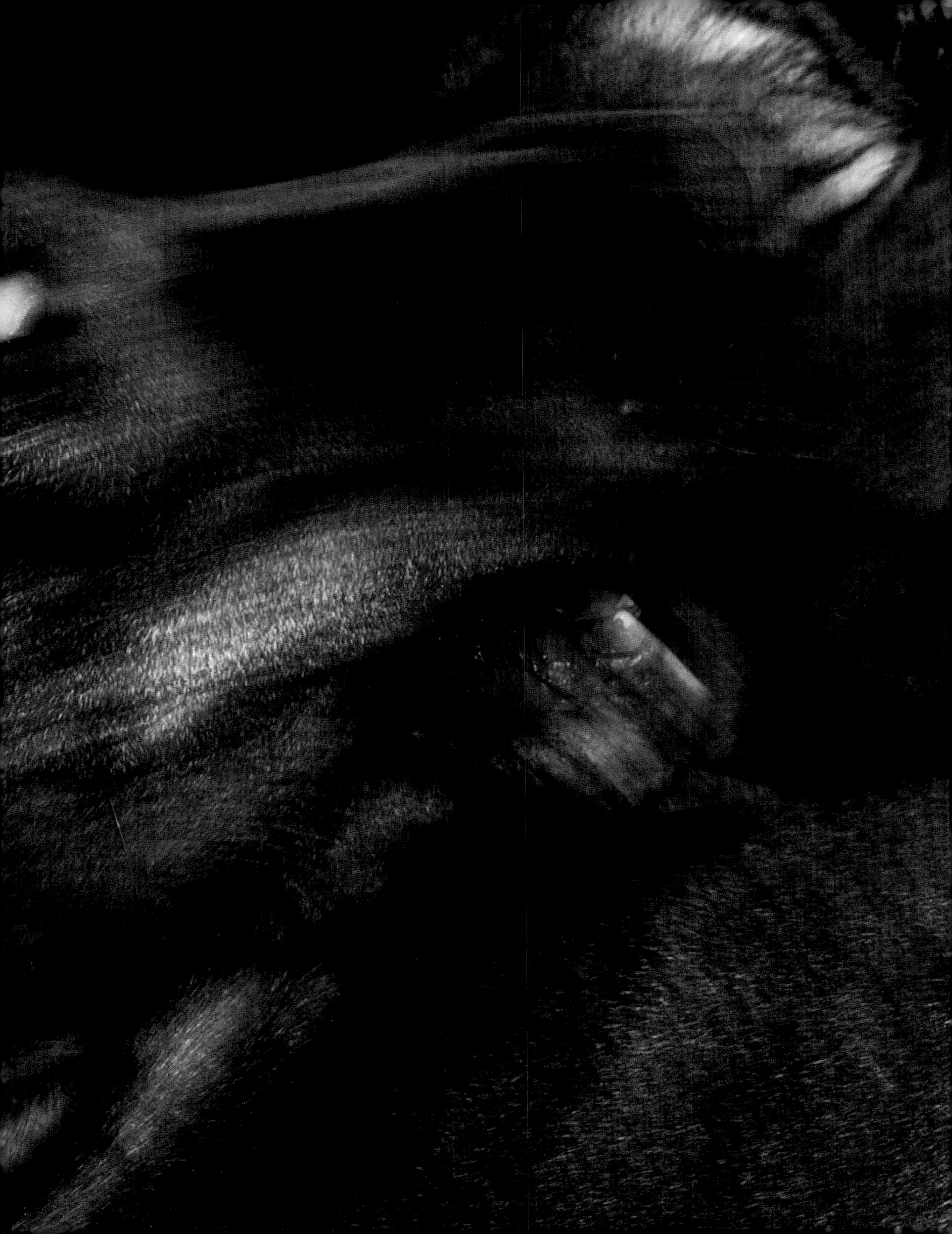

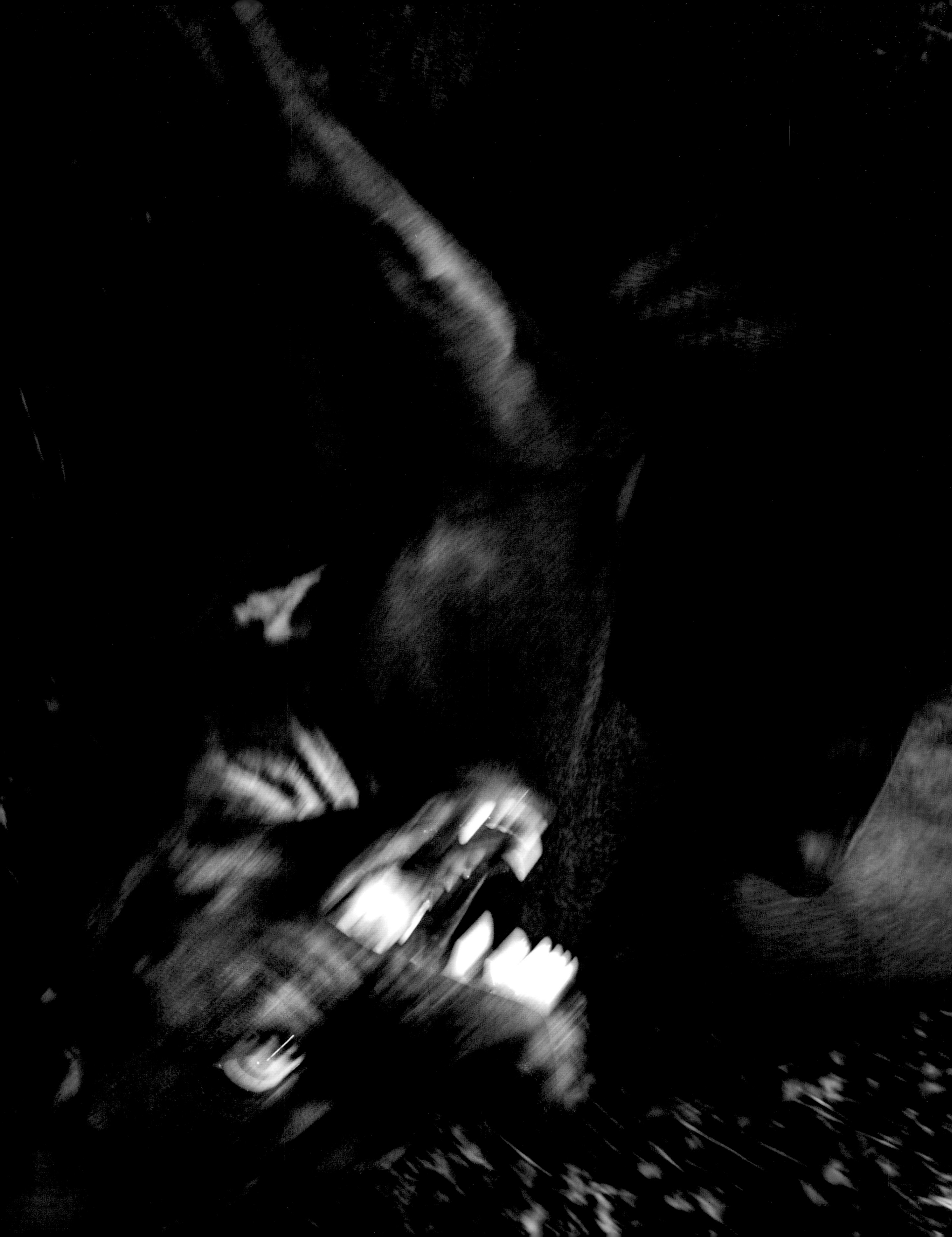

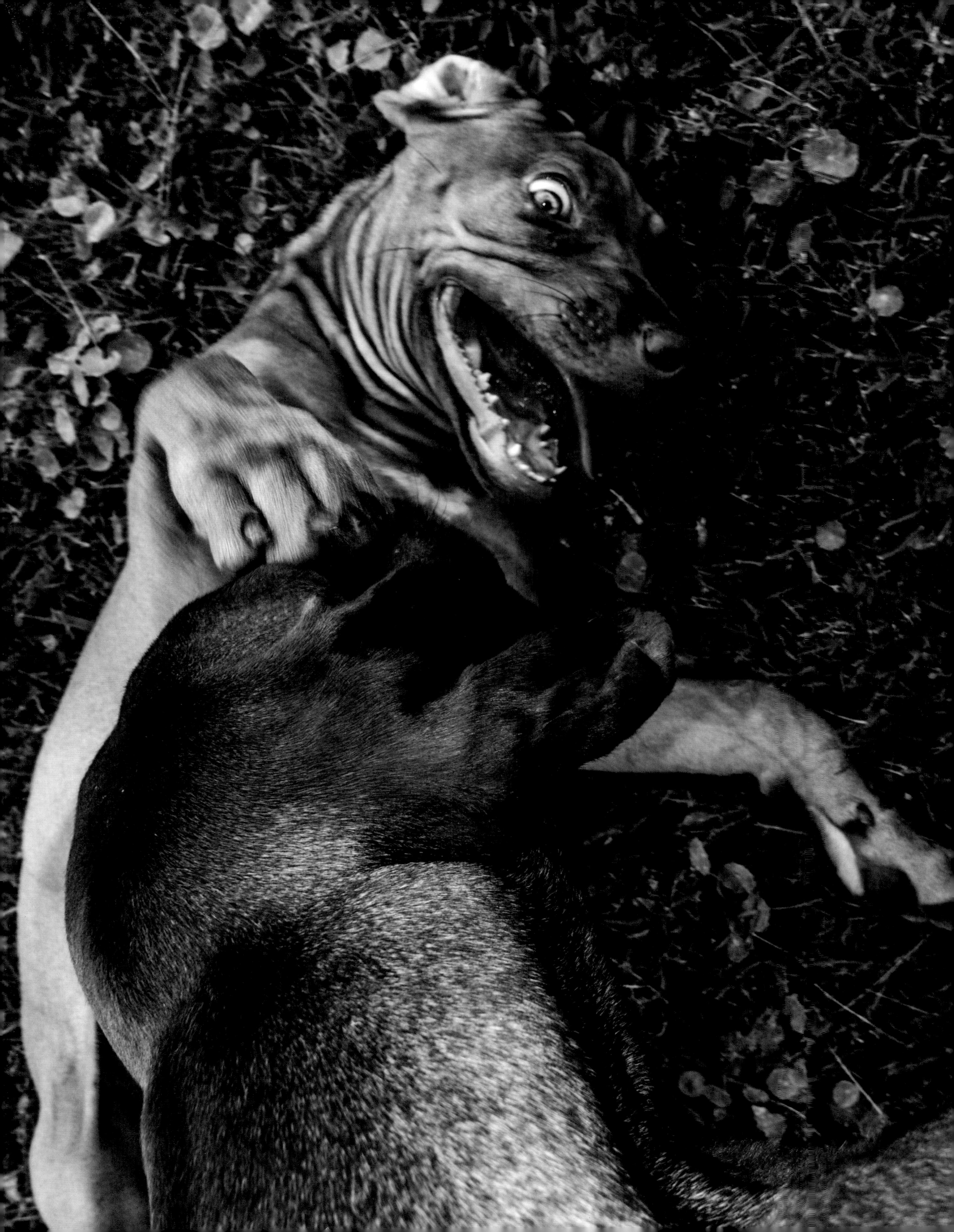

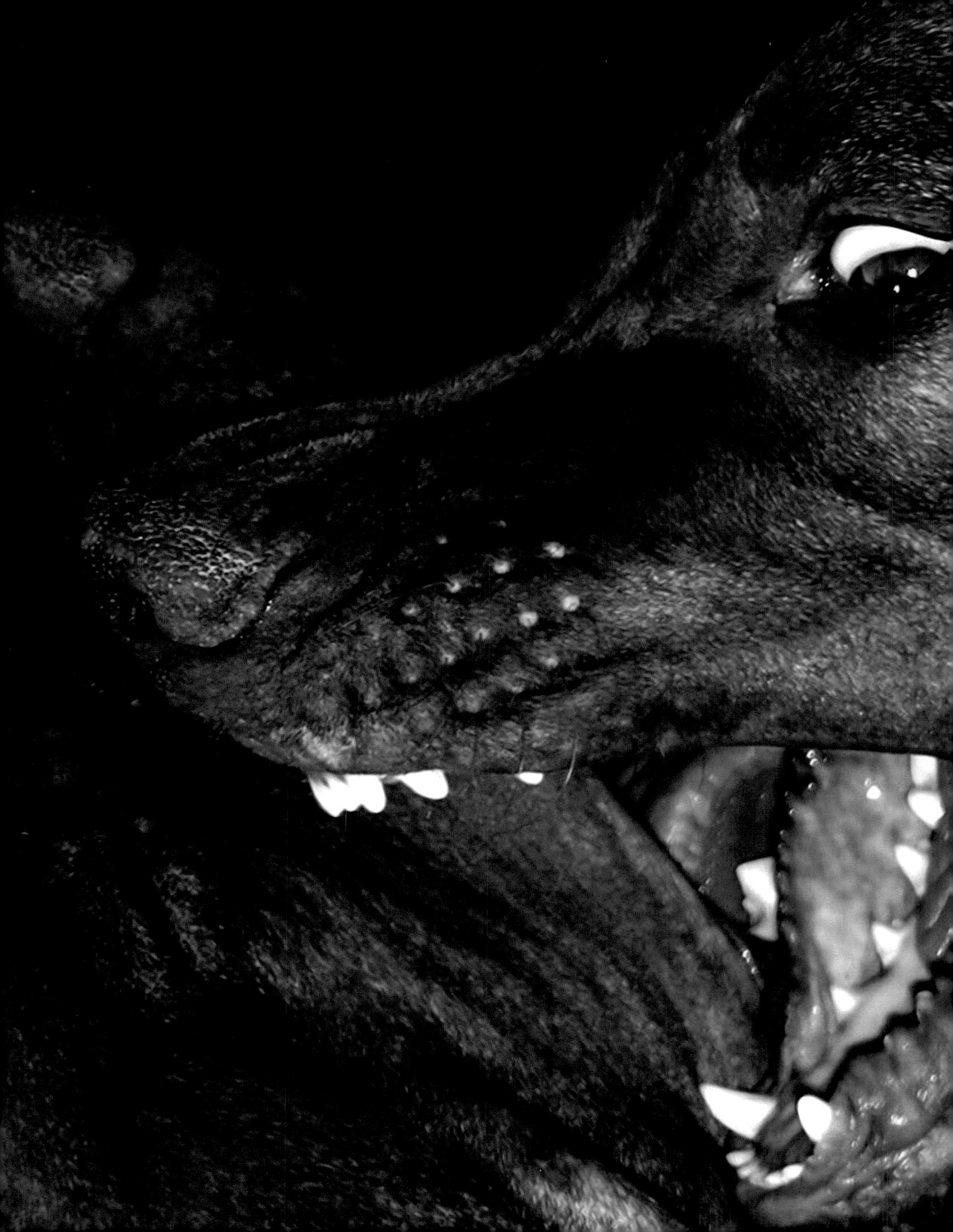

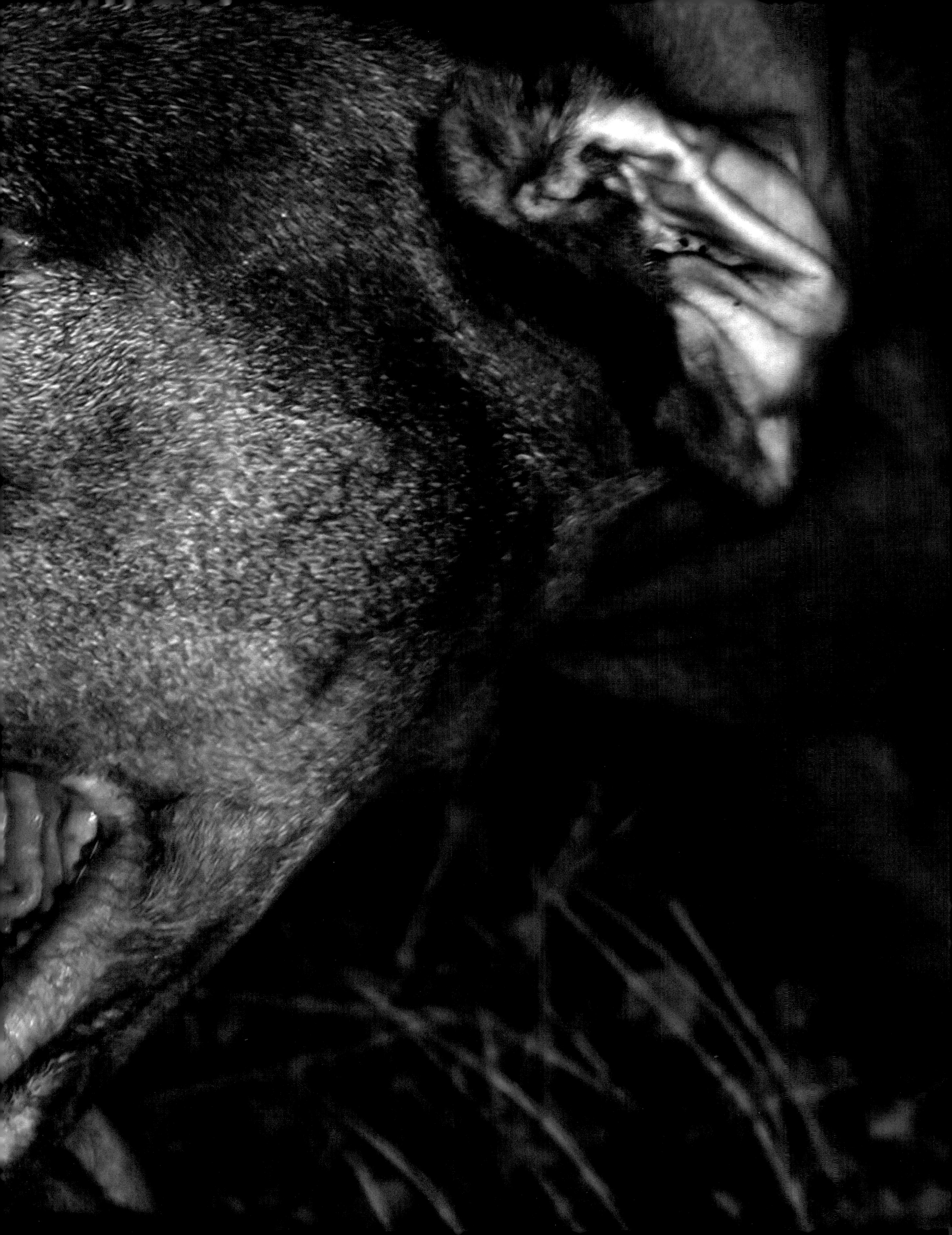

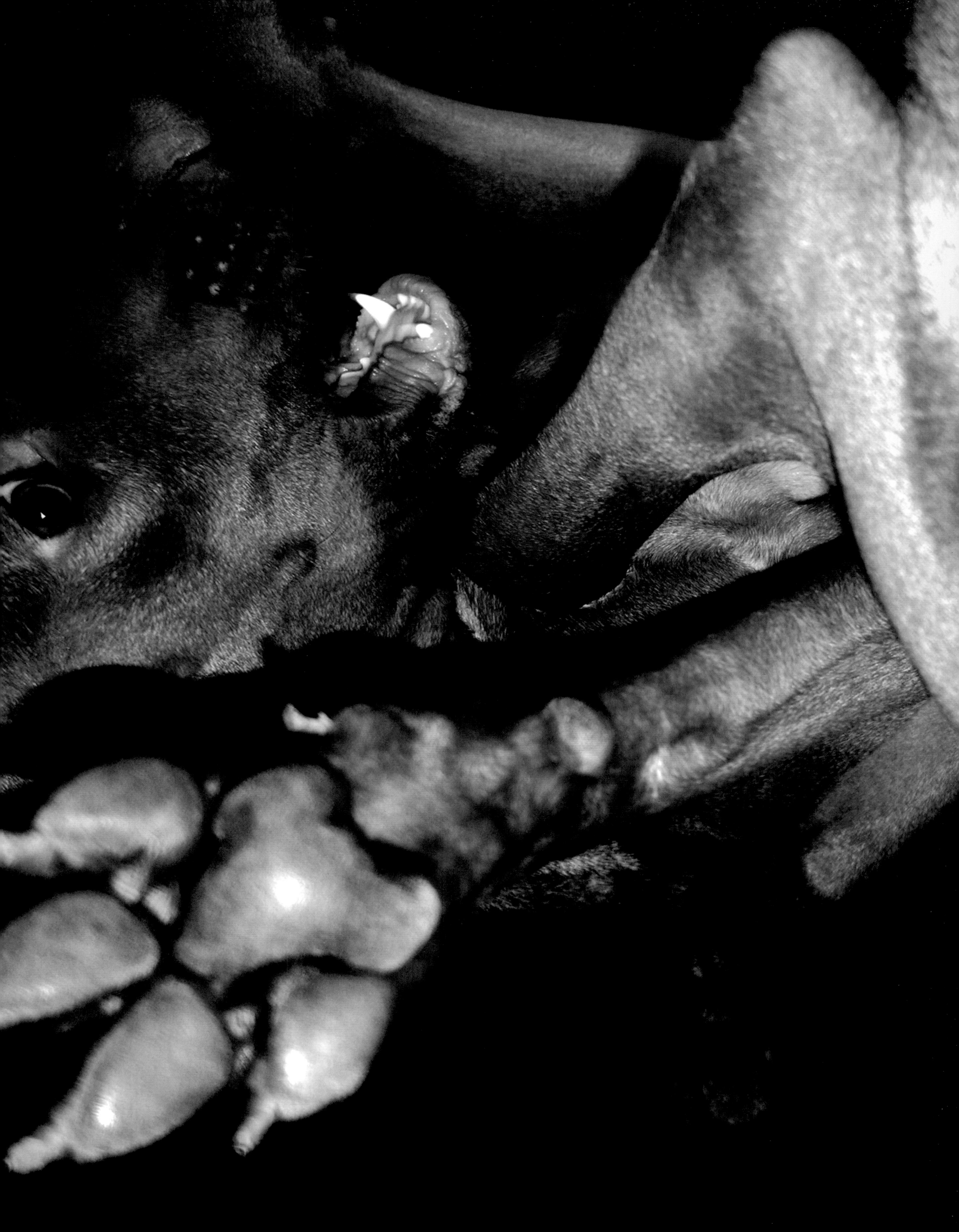

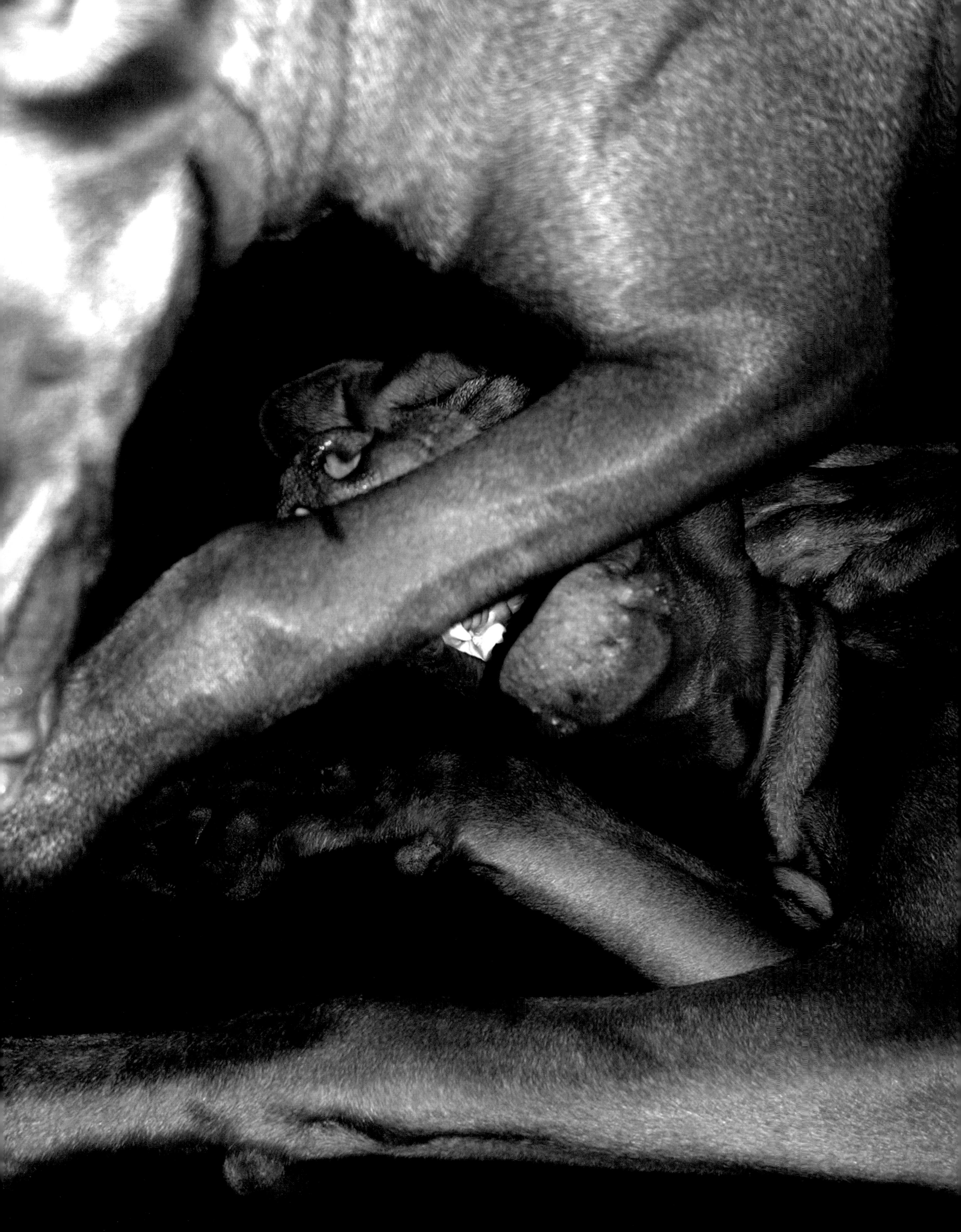

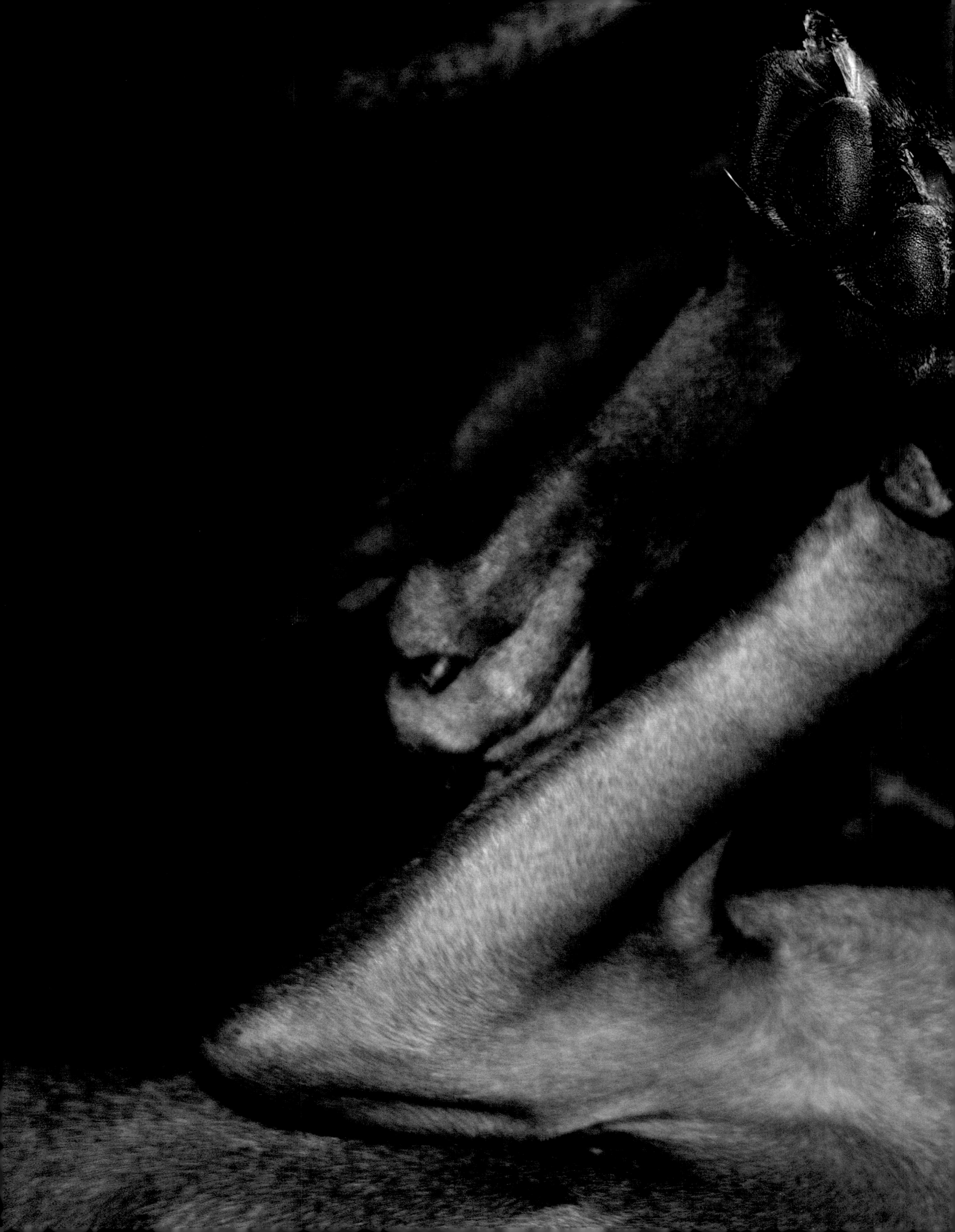

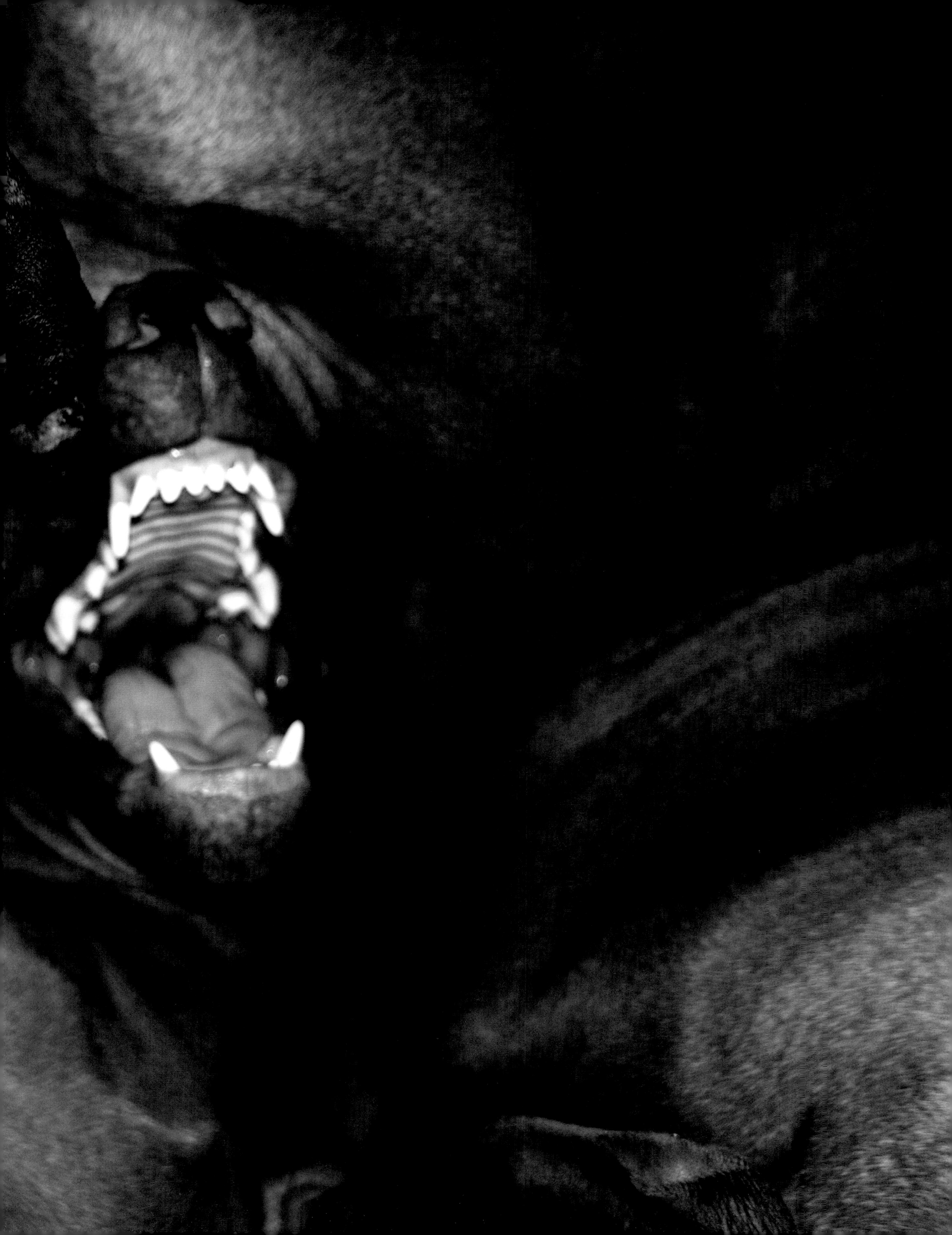

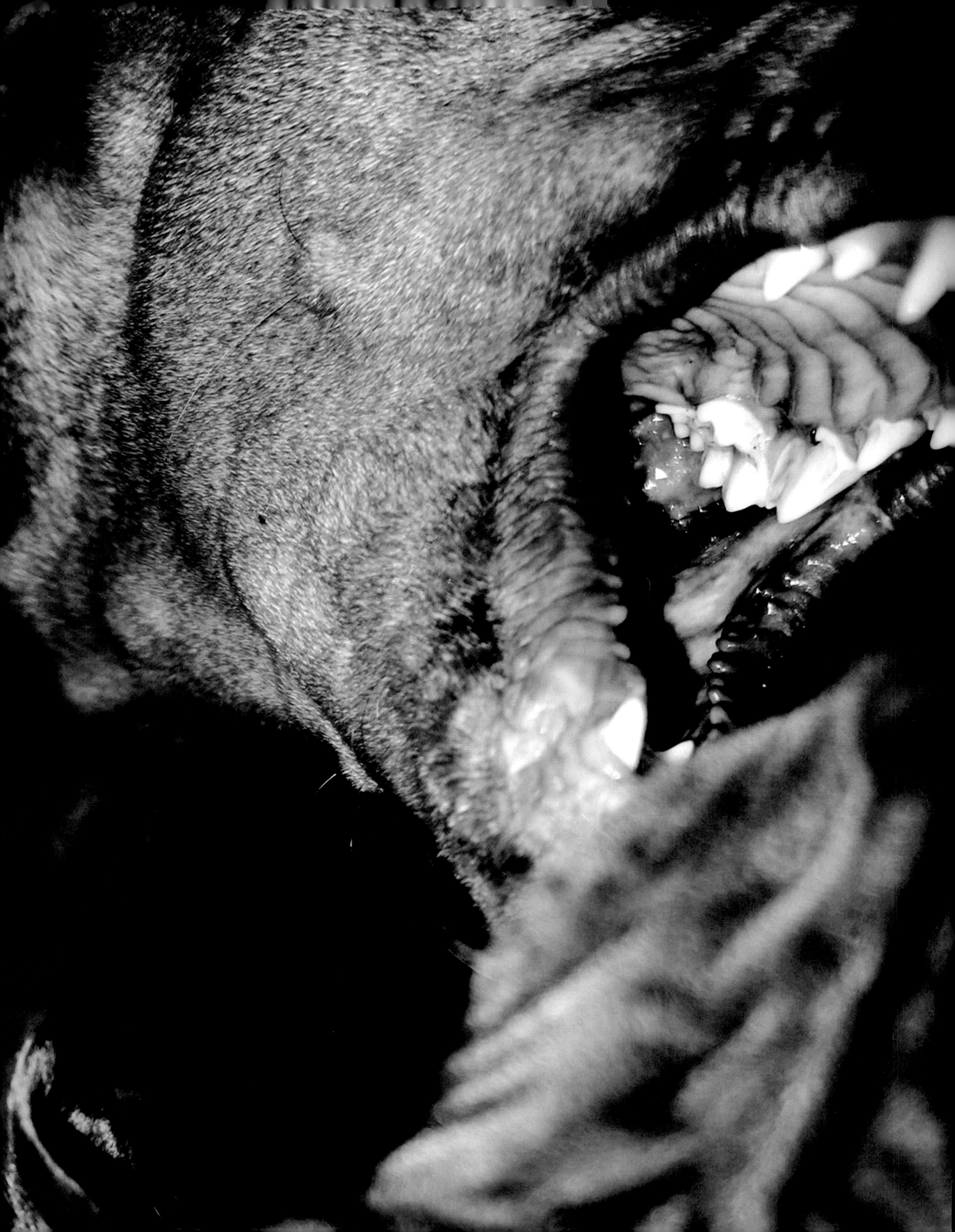

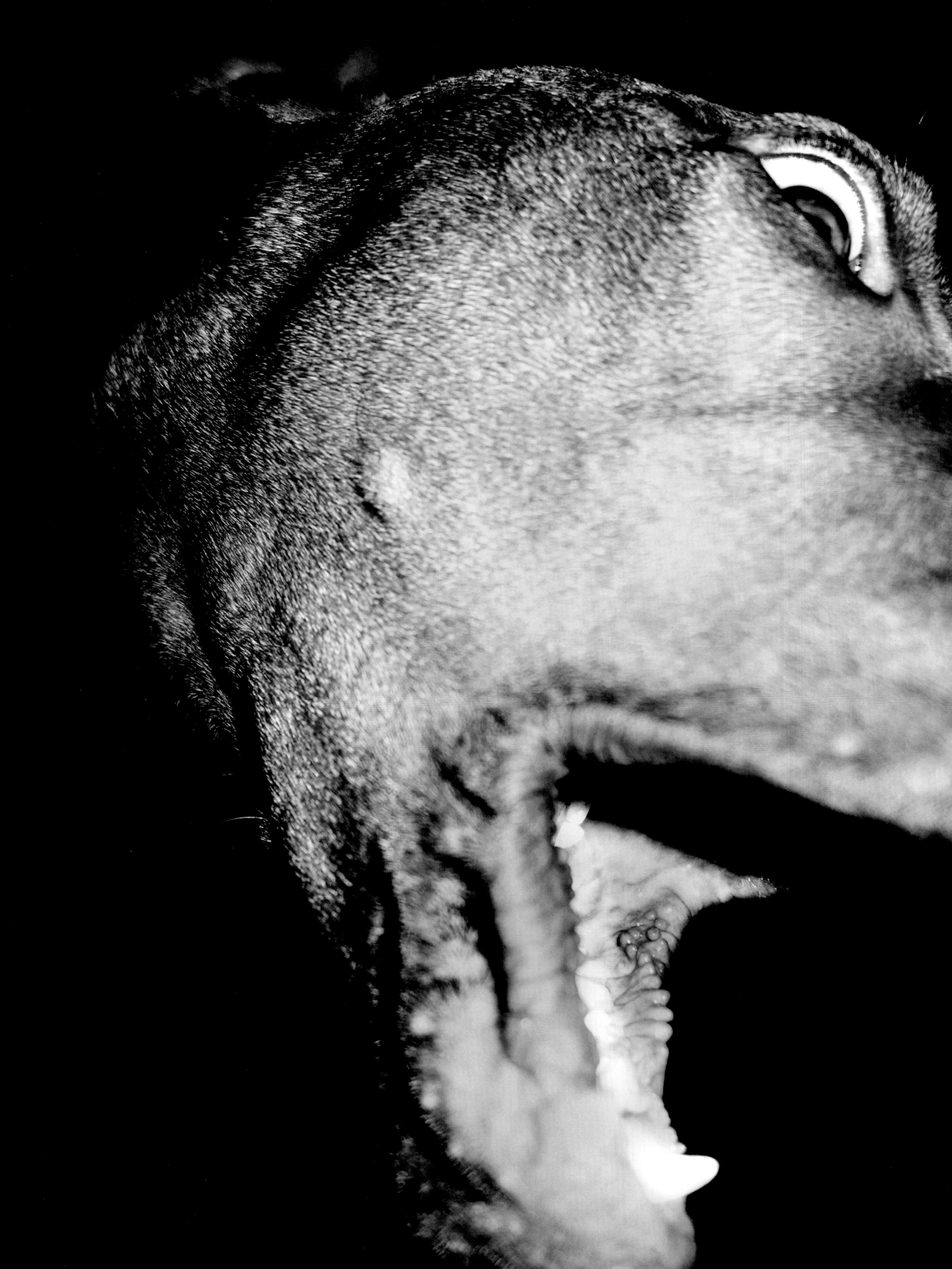

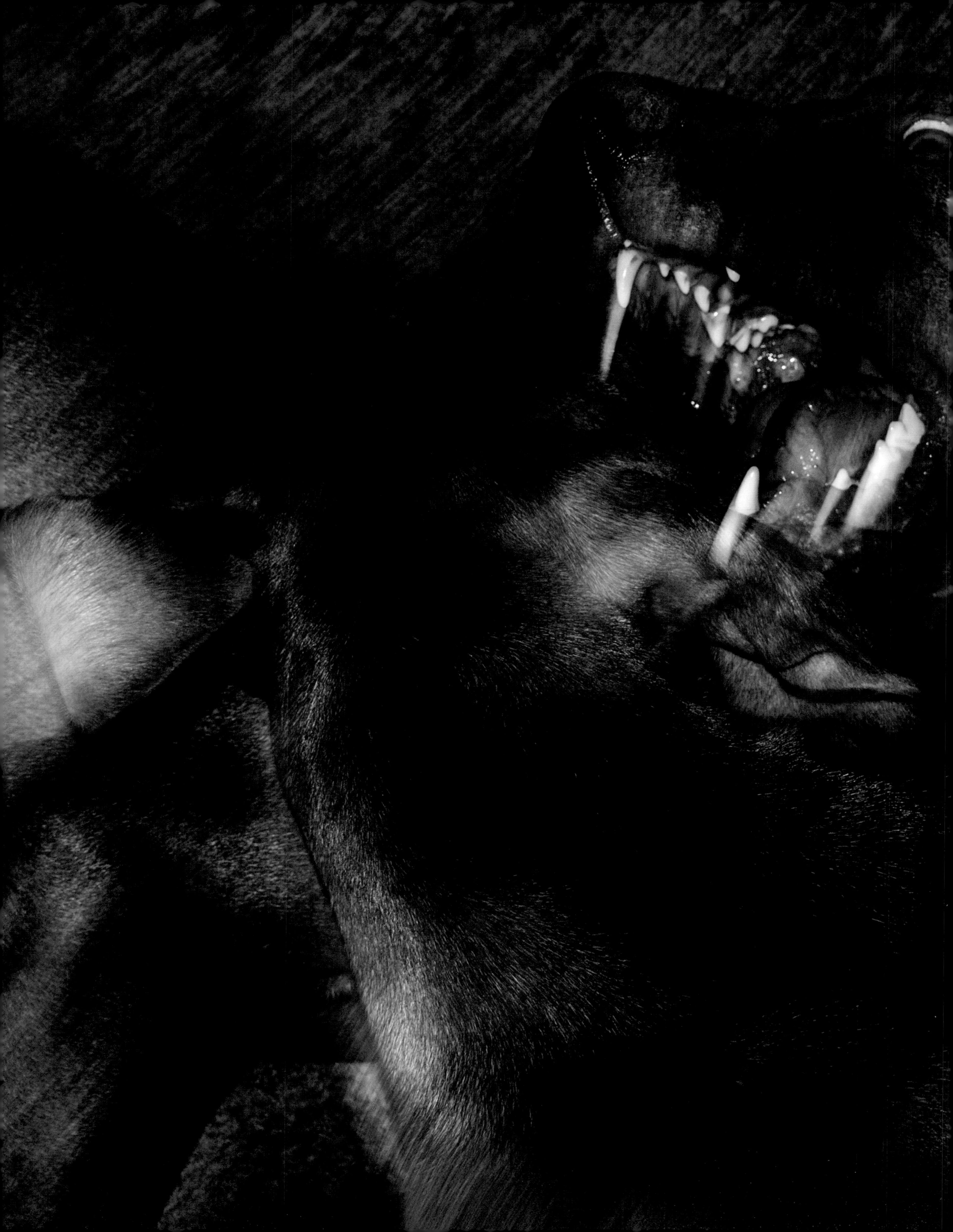

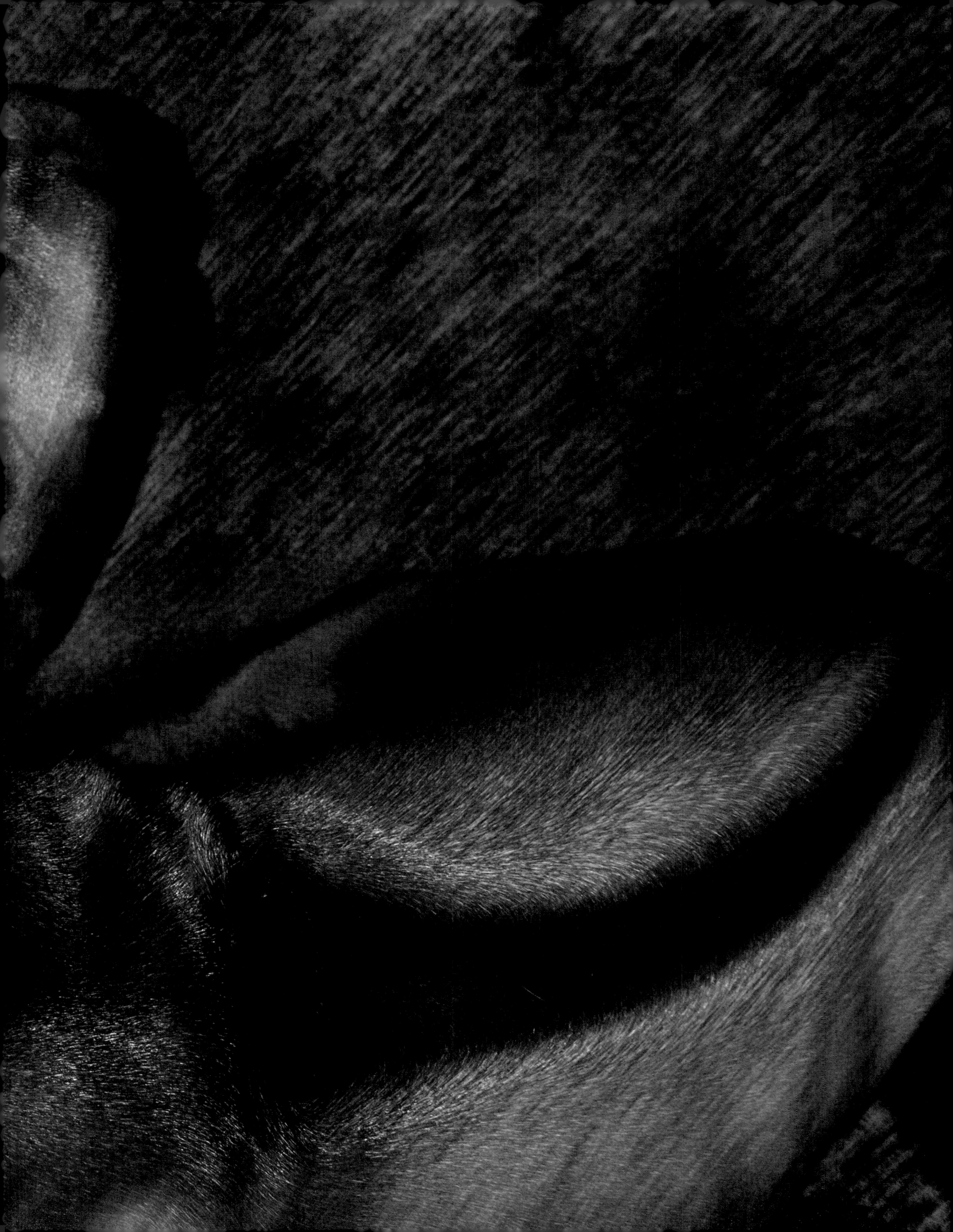

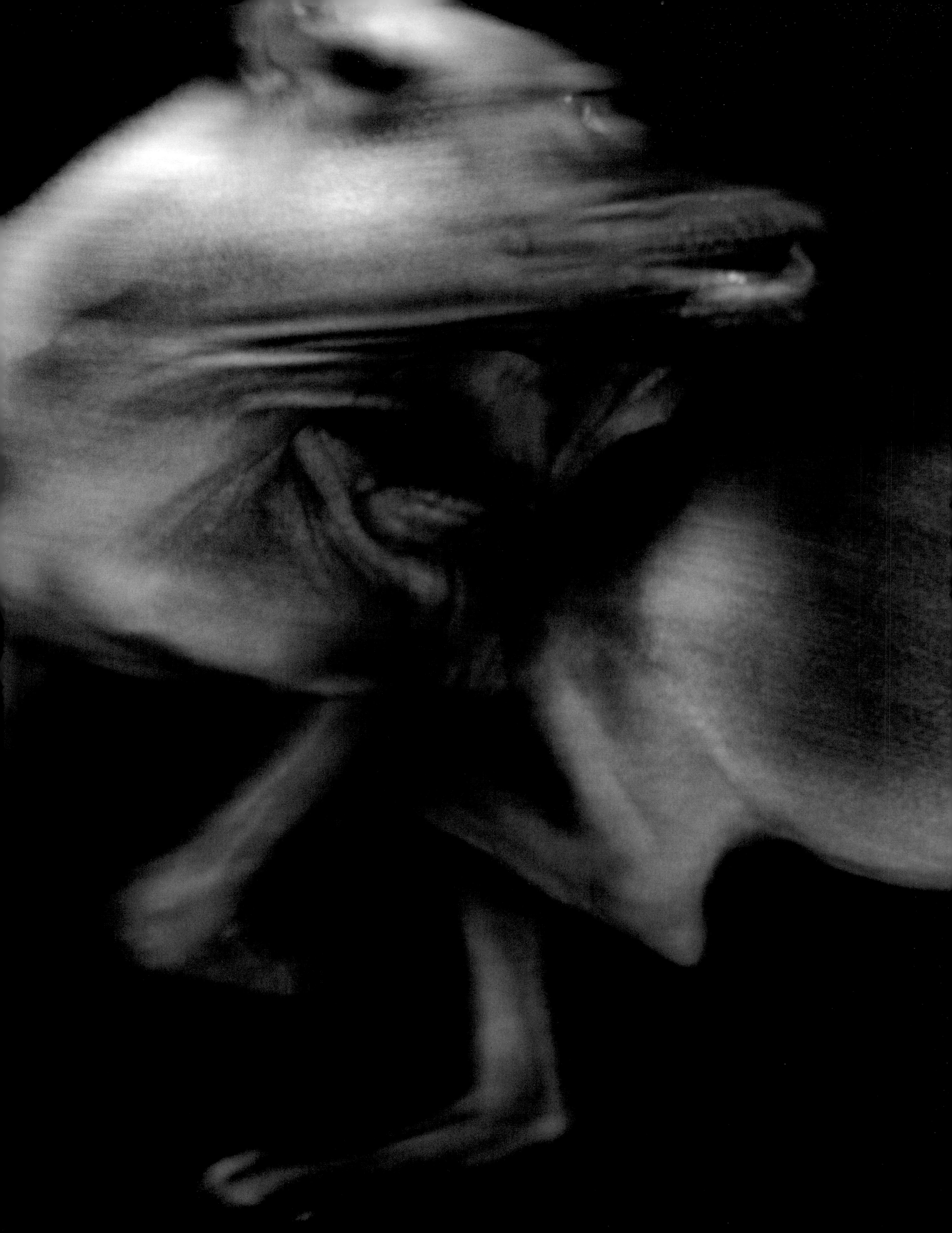

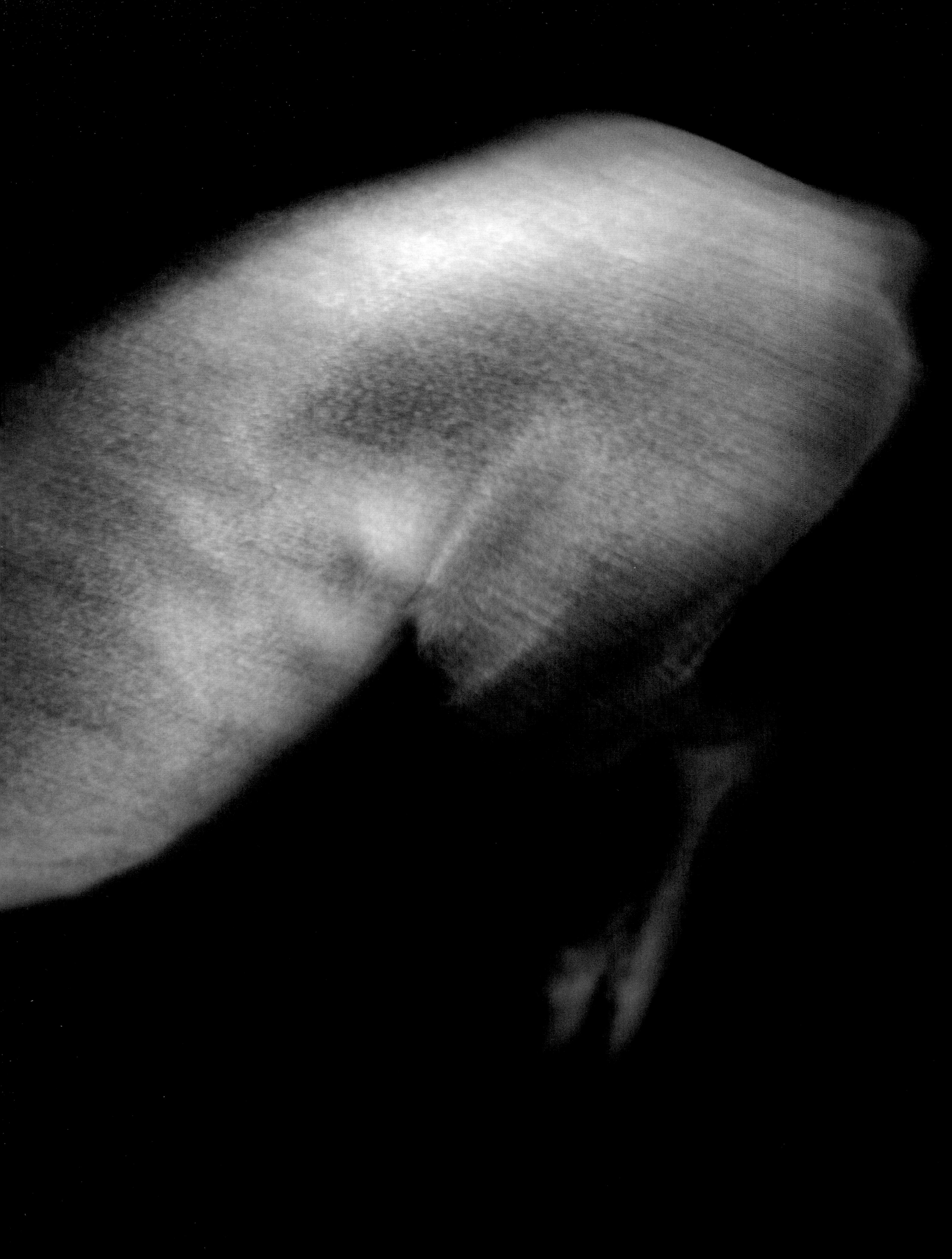

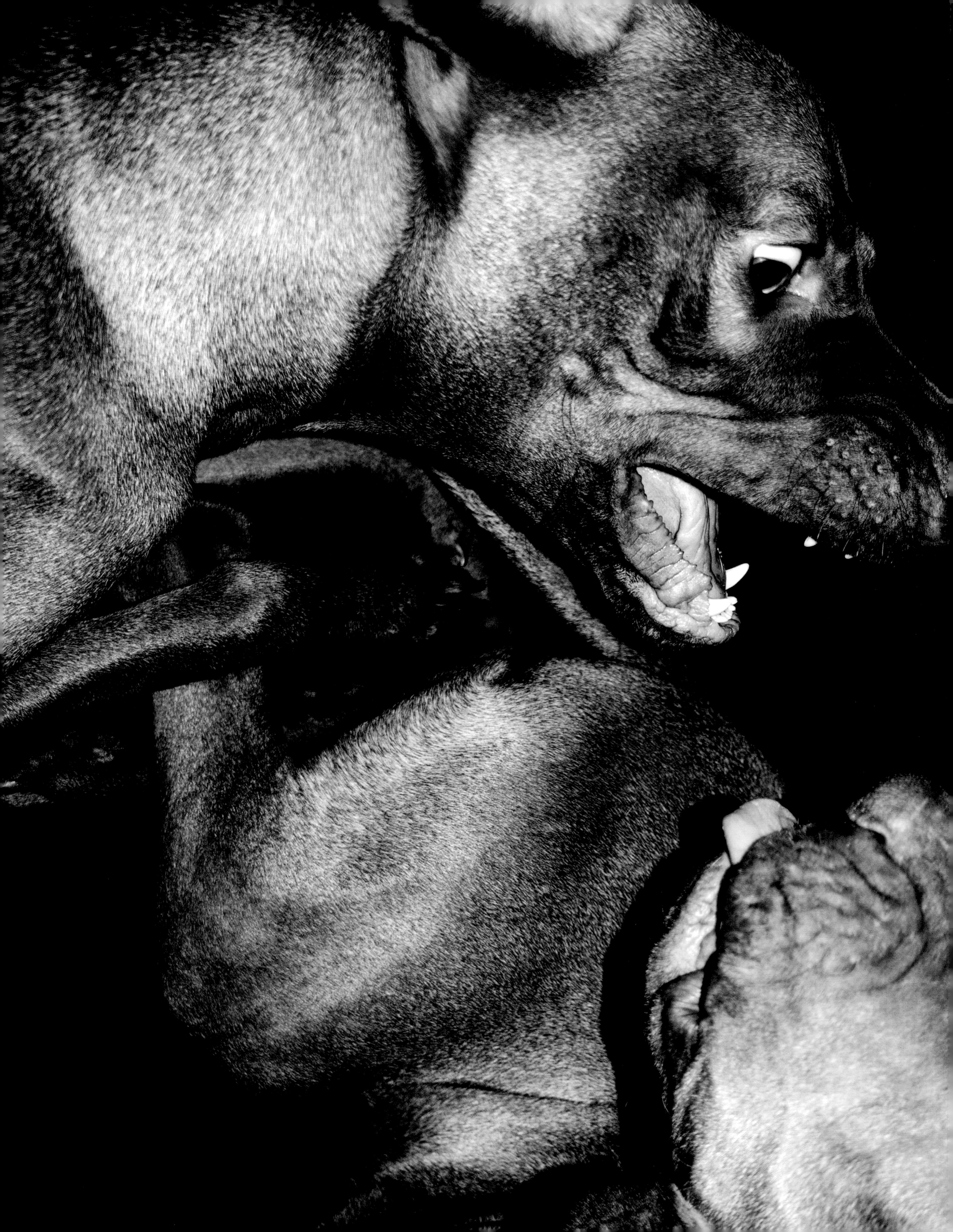

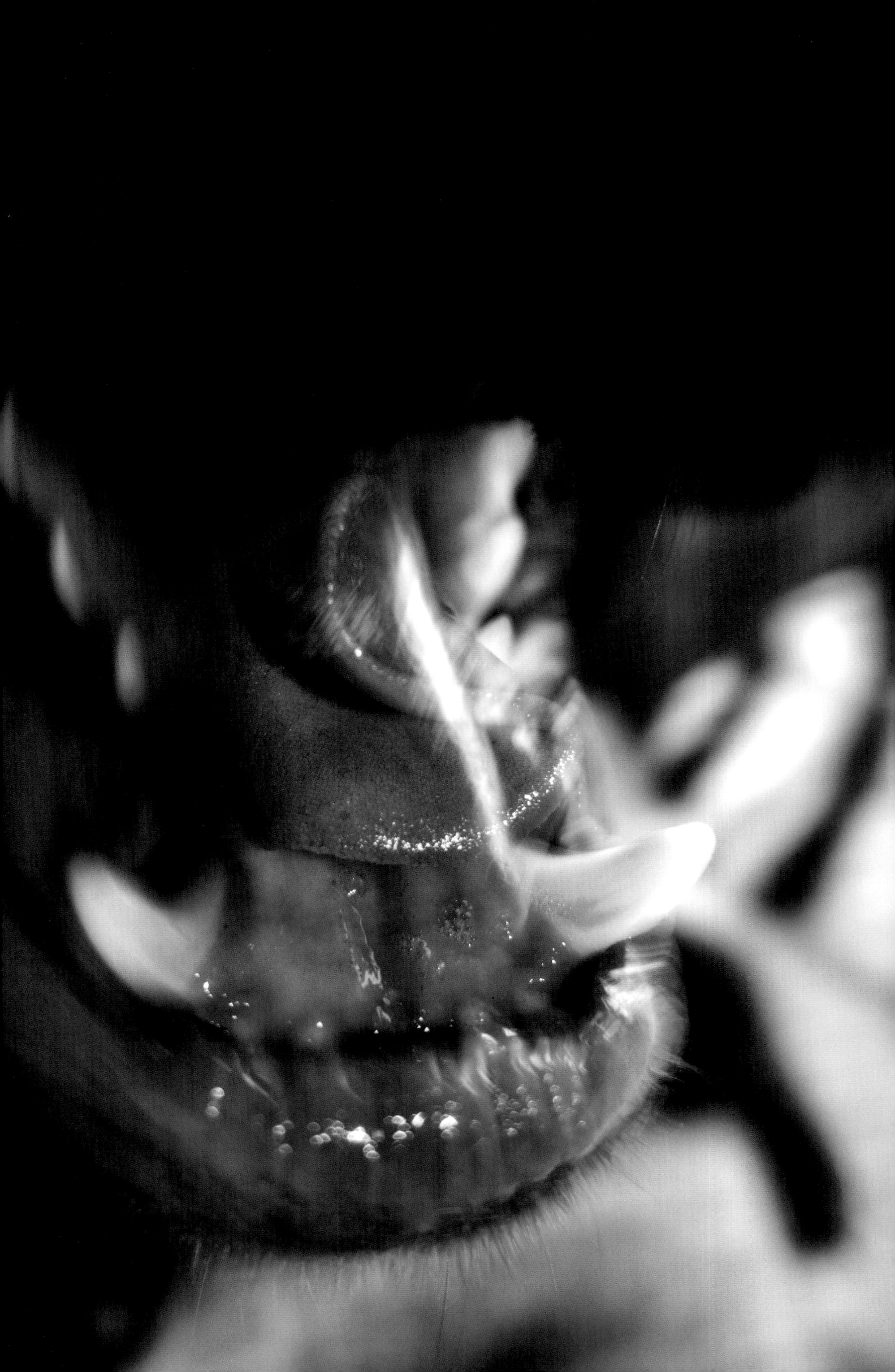

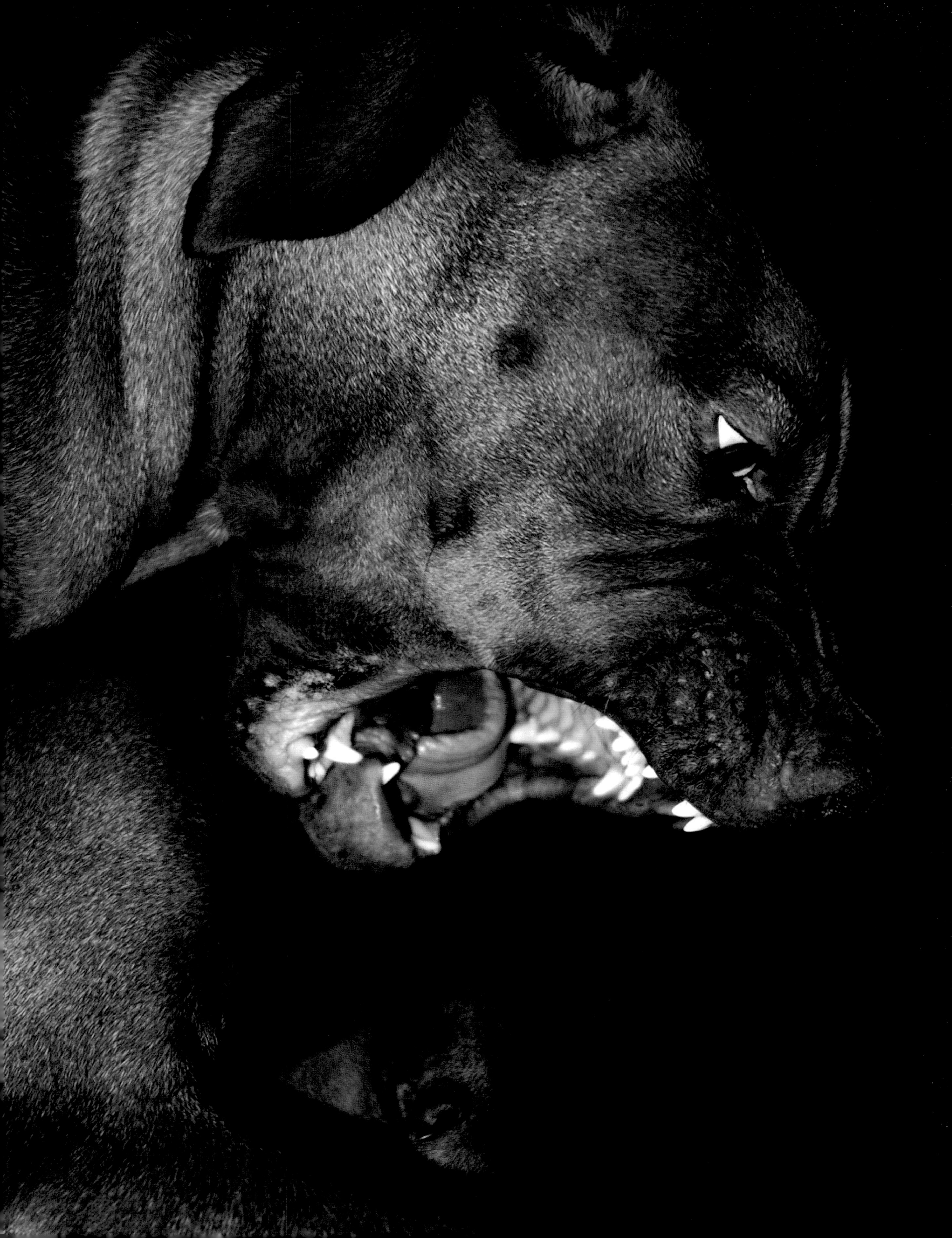

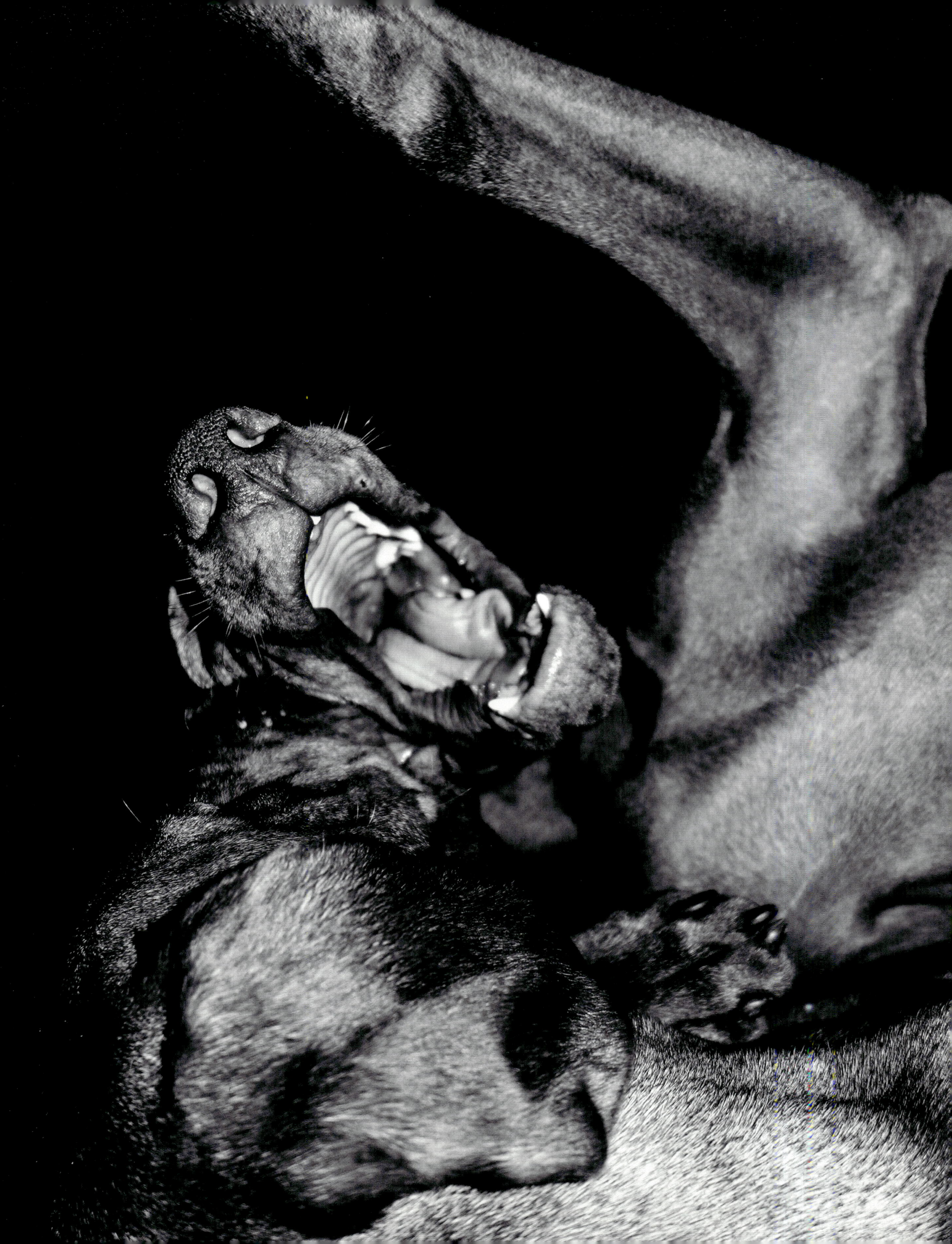

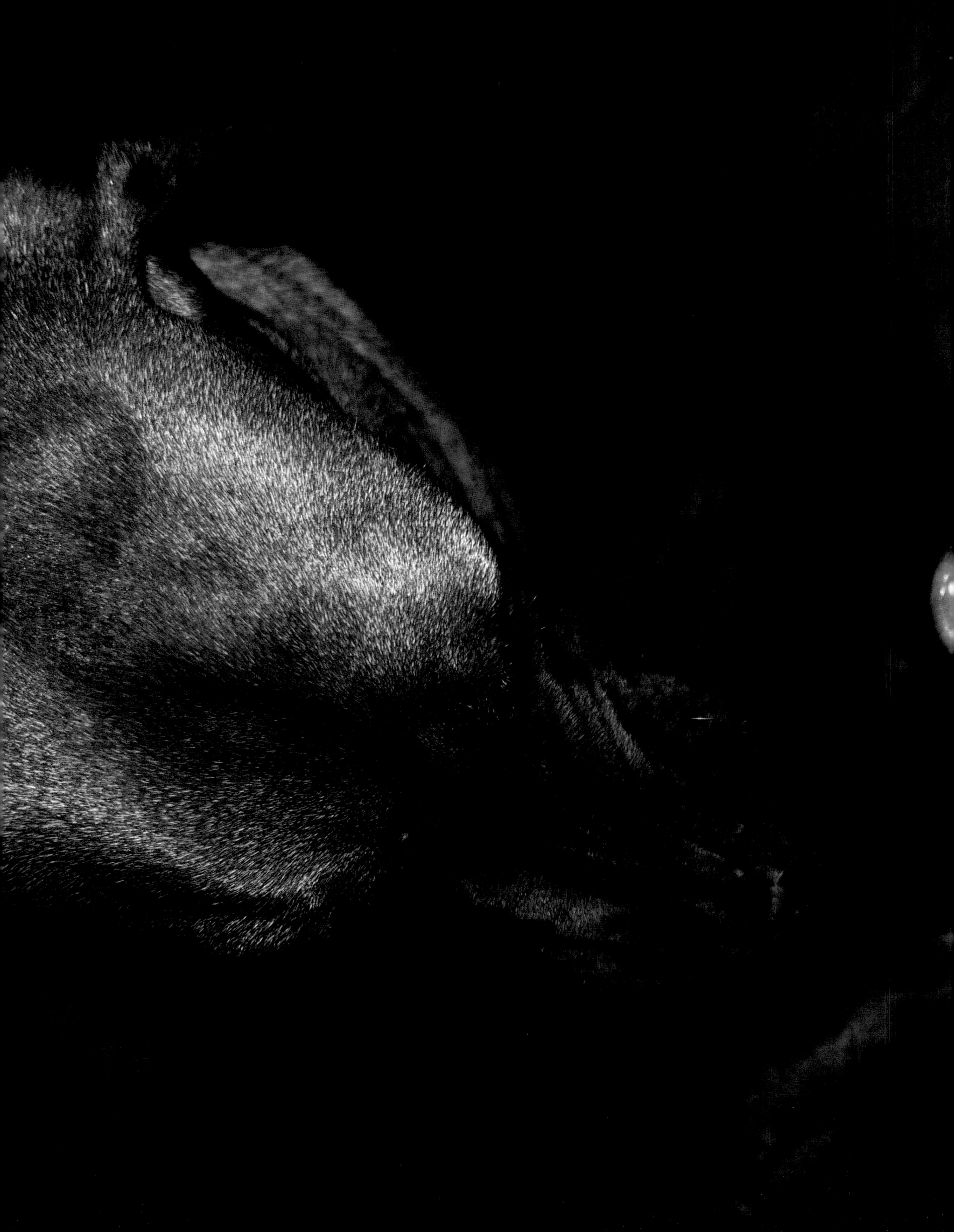

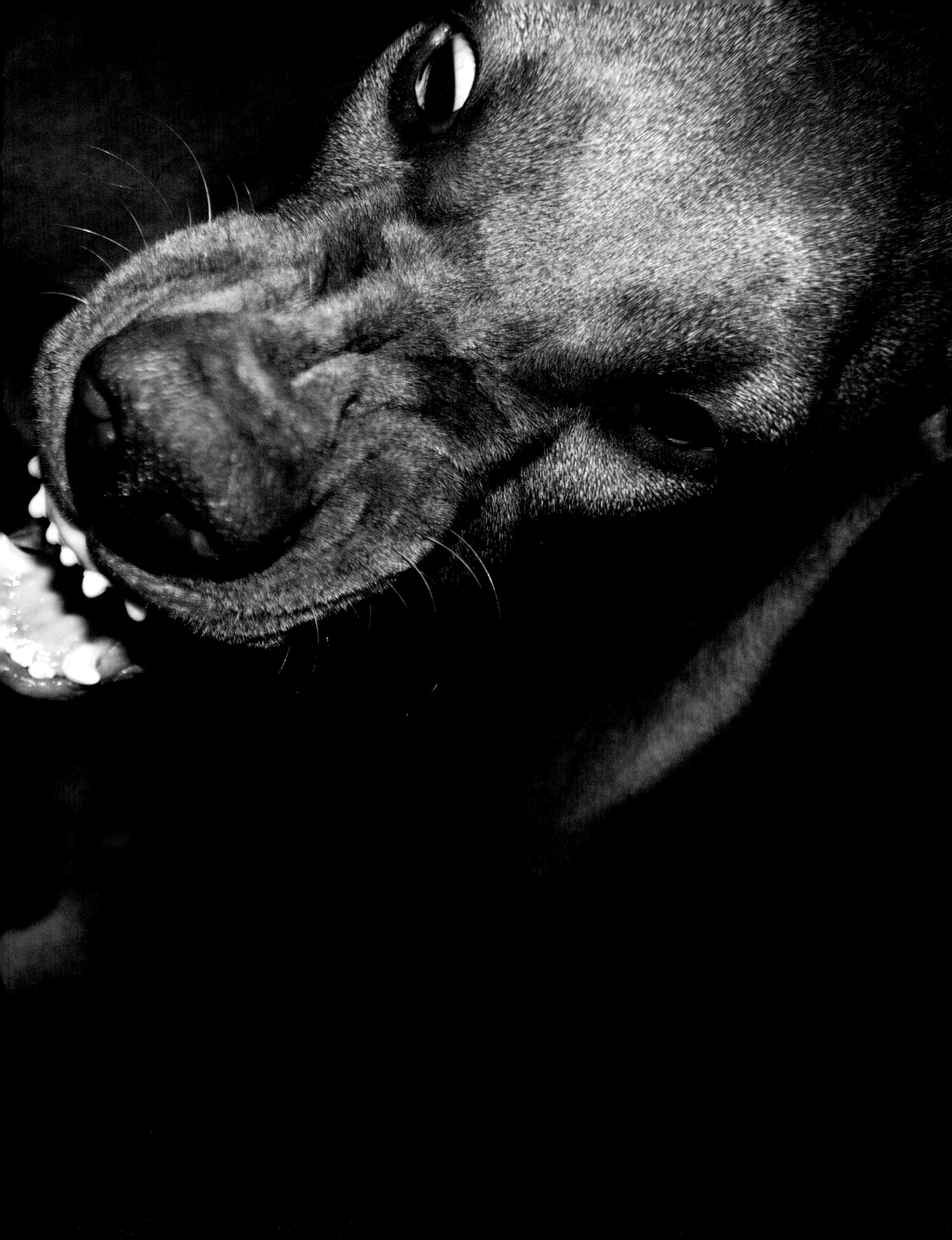

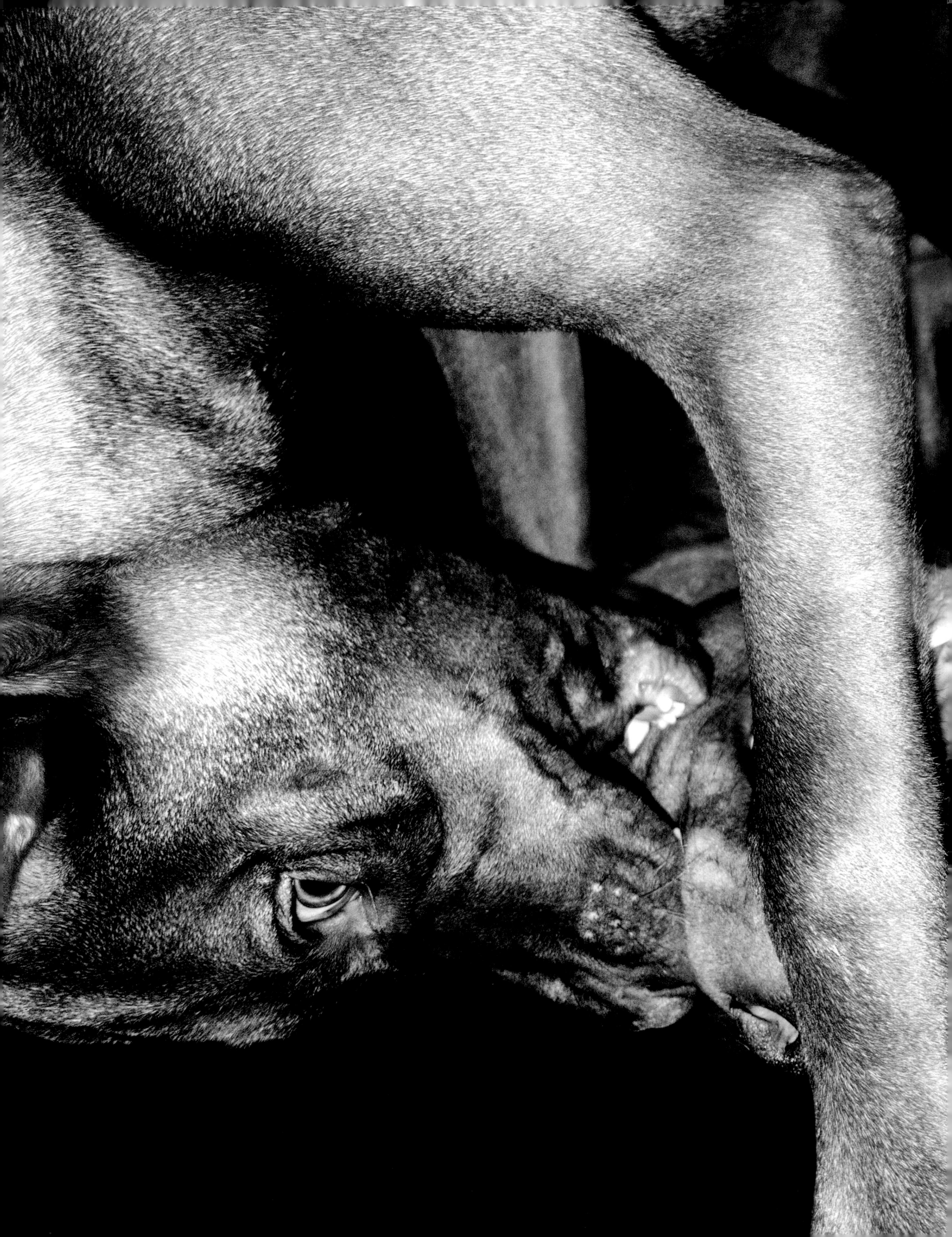

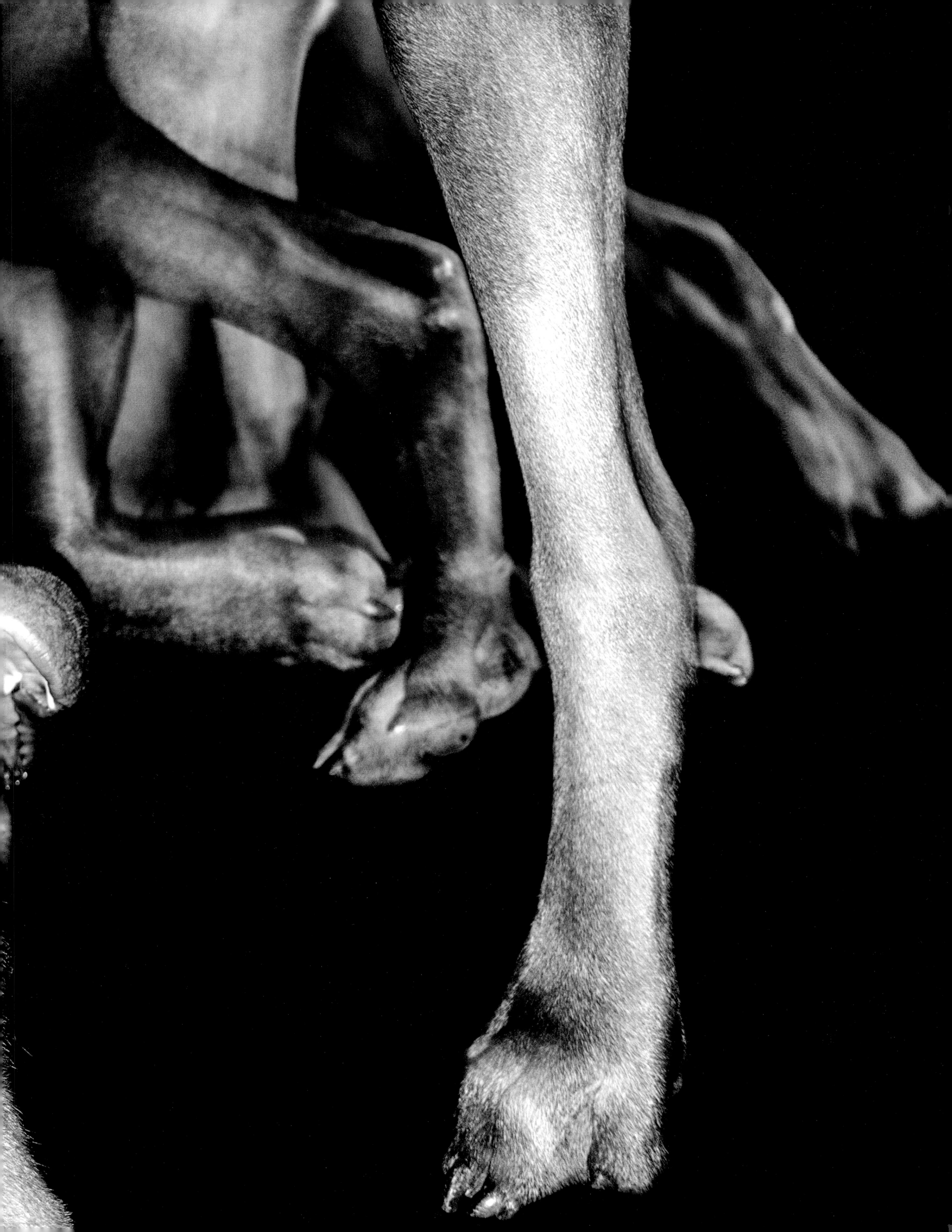

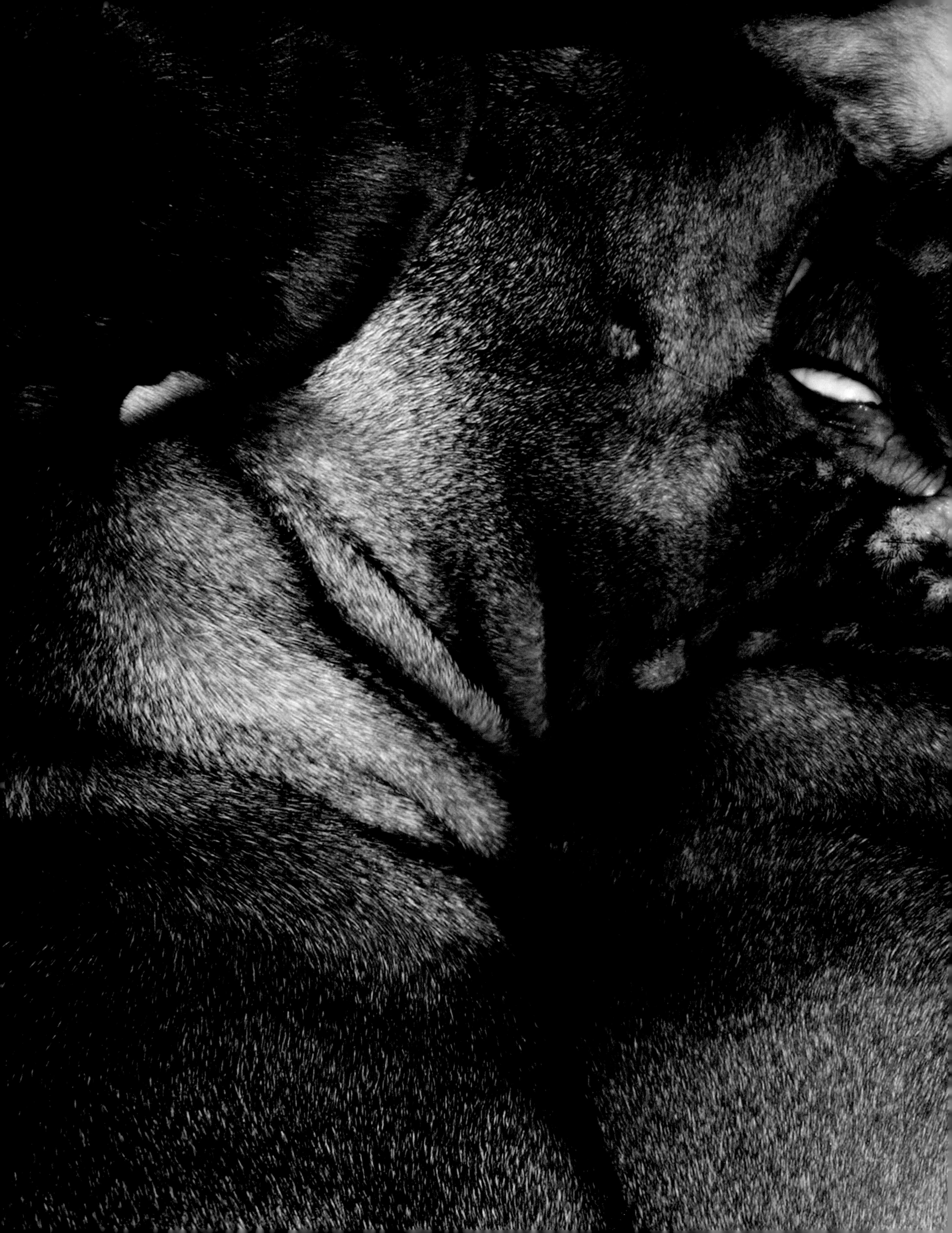

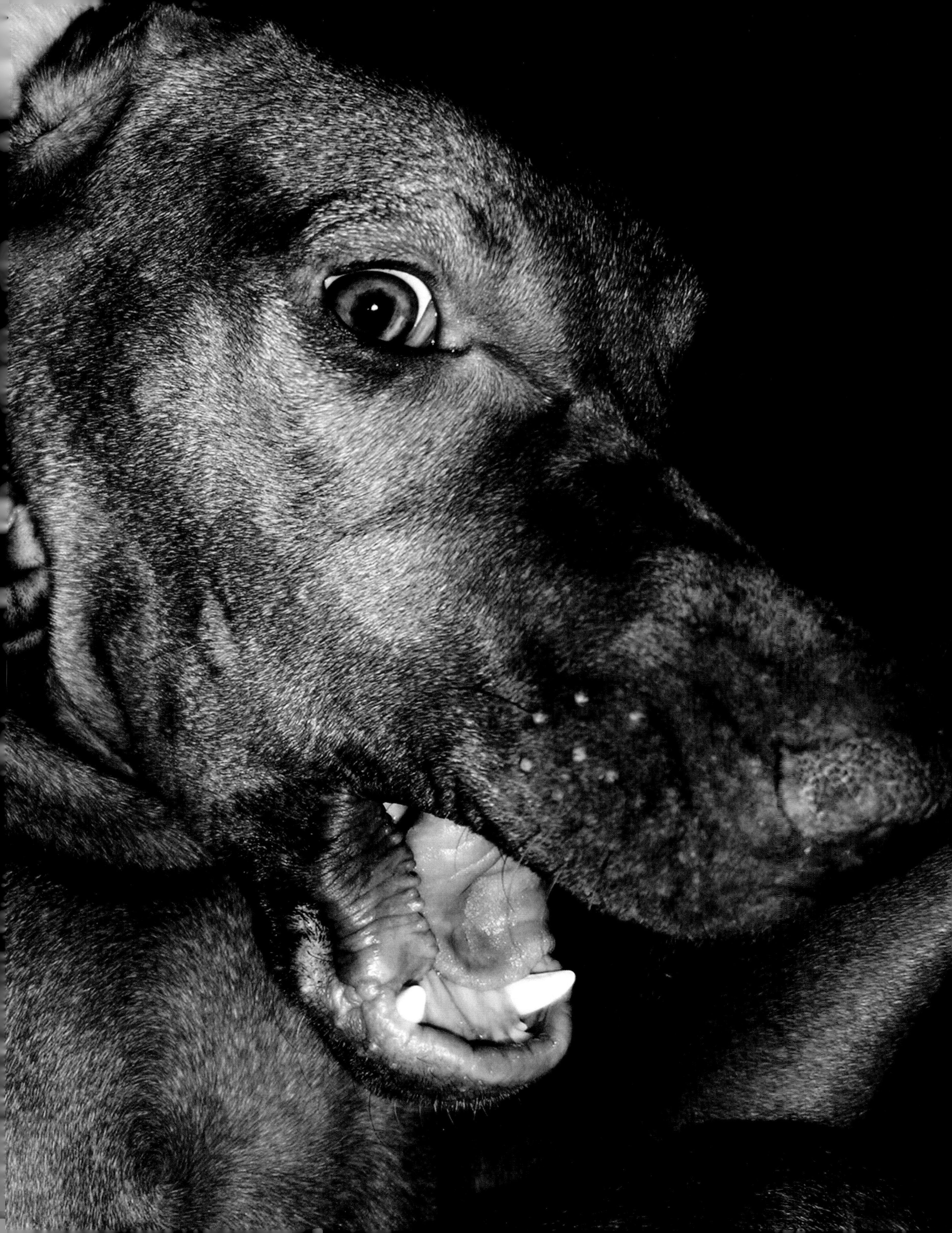

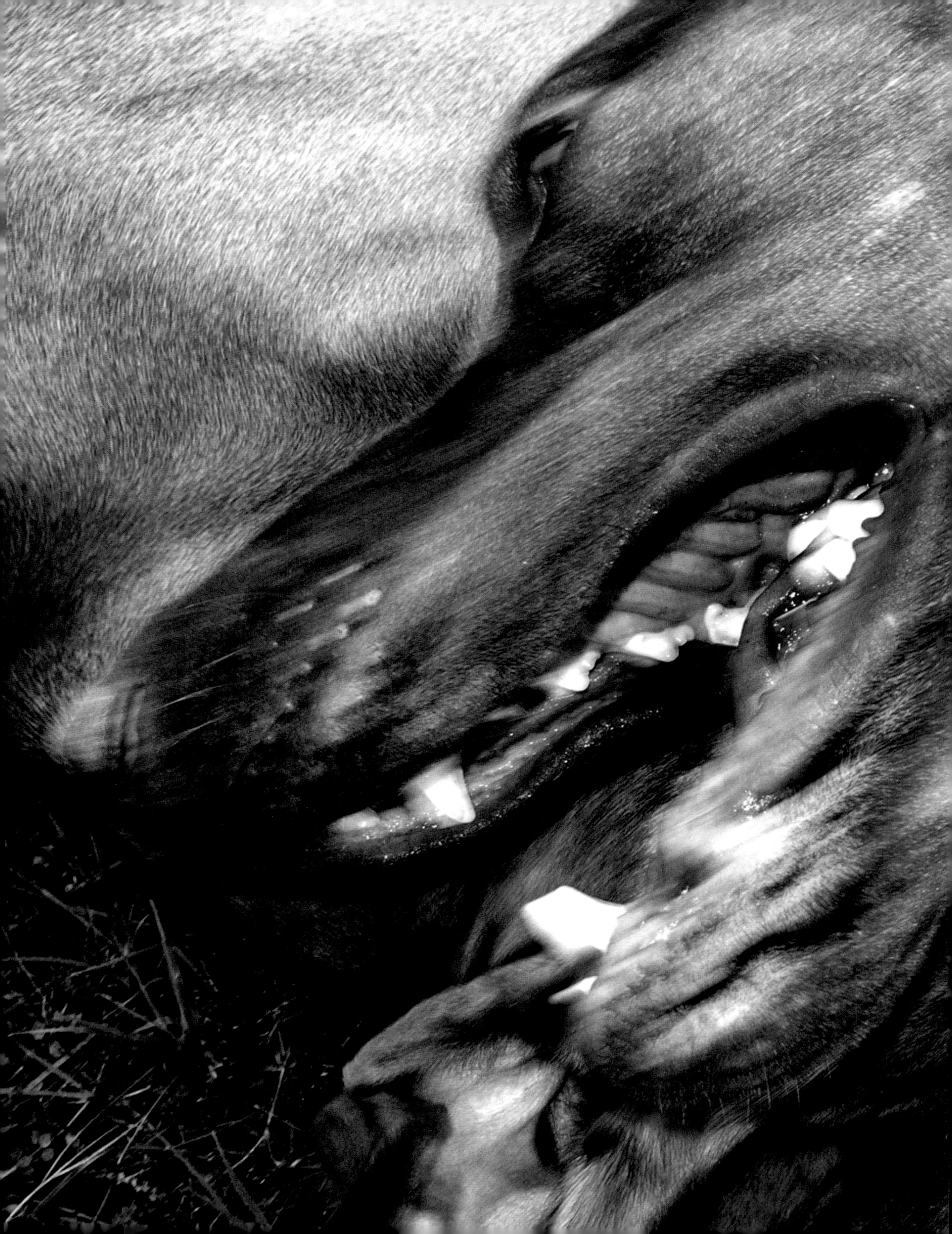

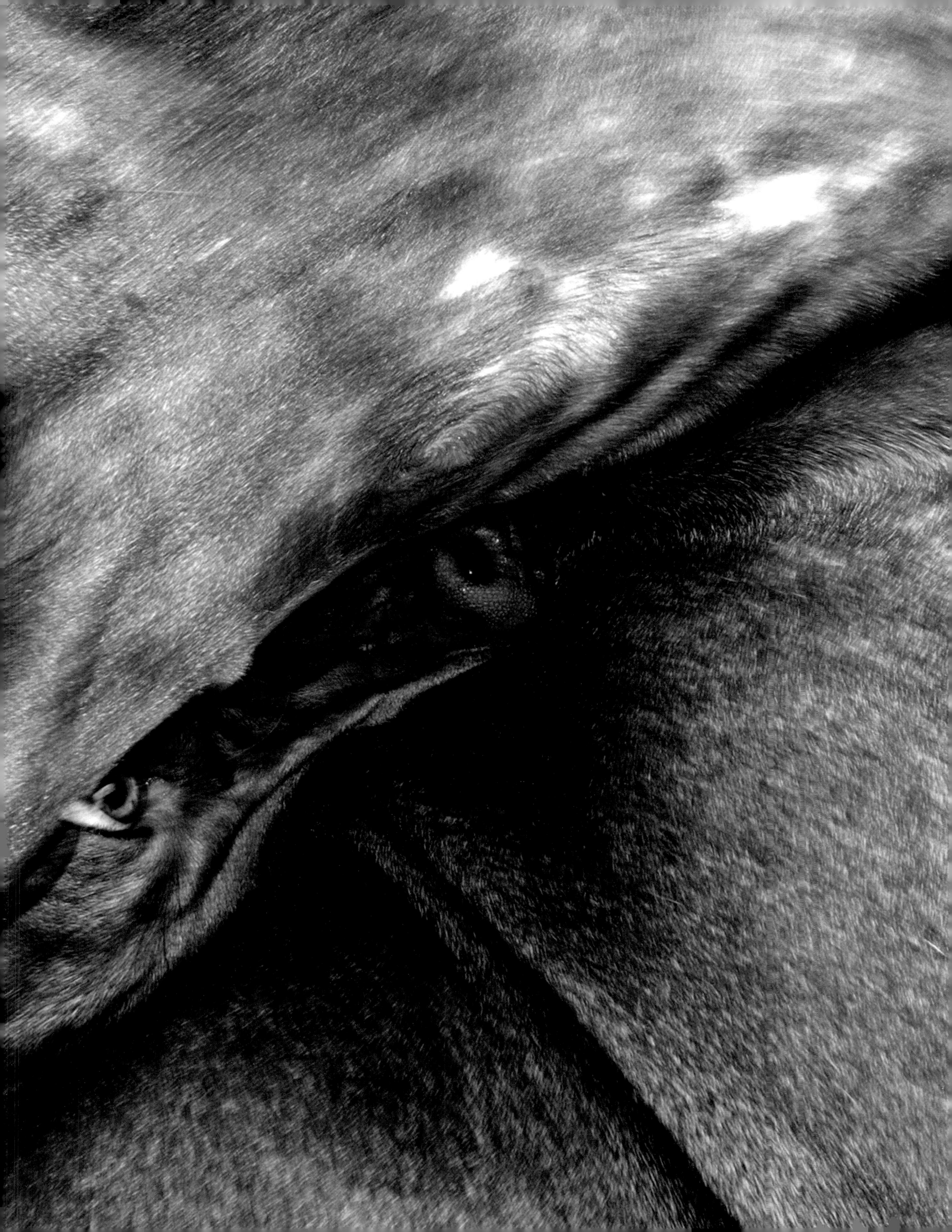

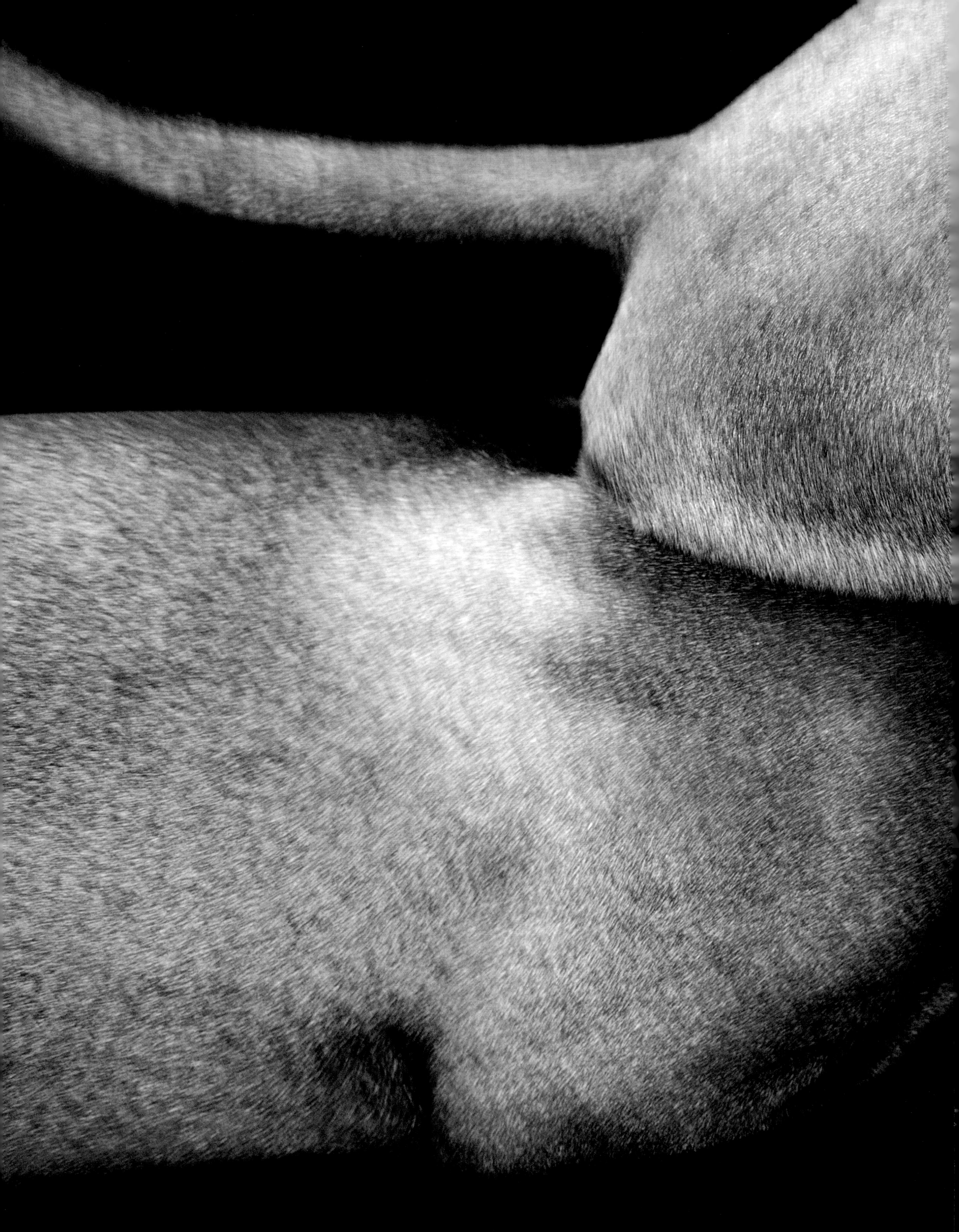

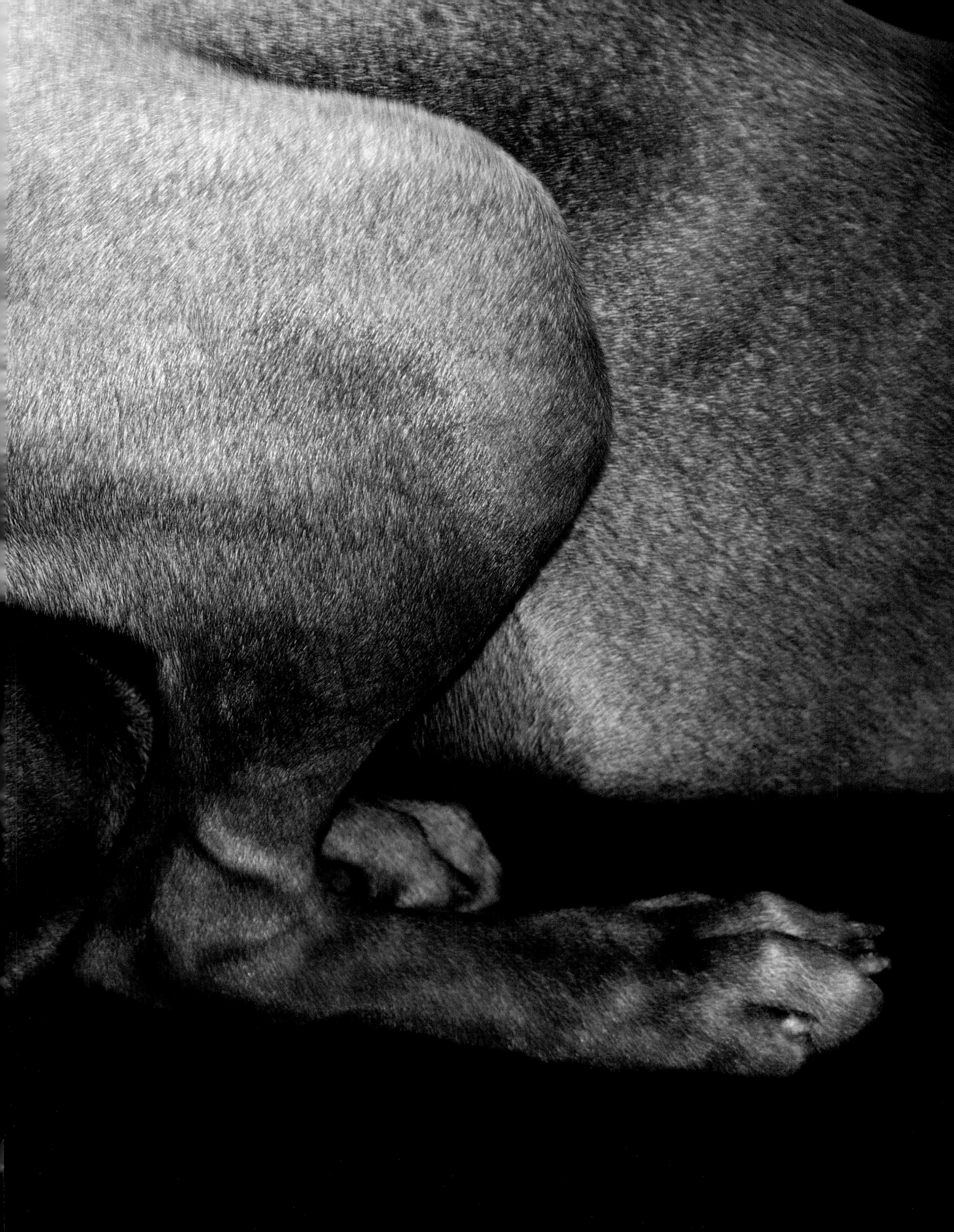

This publication was produced on the occasion of the exhibition *Charles and Saatchi*, *The Dogs*
at Galerie Gmurzynska, Art Basel Miami Beach

galerie gmurzynska

CHARLES AND SAATCHI, THE DOGS
Jean Pigozzi

BOOK DESIGN BY YOLANDA CUOMO DESIGN, NYC
Associate Designer: Bonnie Briant
Assistant Designer: Bobbie Richardson

Published by Damiani
info@damianieditore.com
www.damianieditore.com

Printed in October 2017 by Grafiche Damiani–Faenza Group SpA, Italy.

ISBN 978-88-6208-592-2

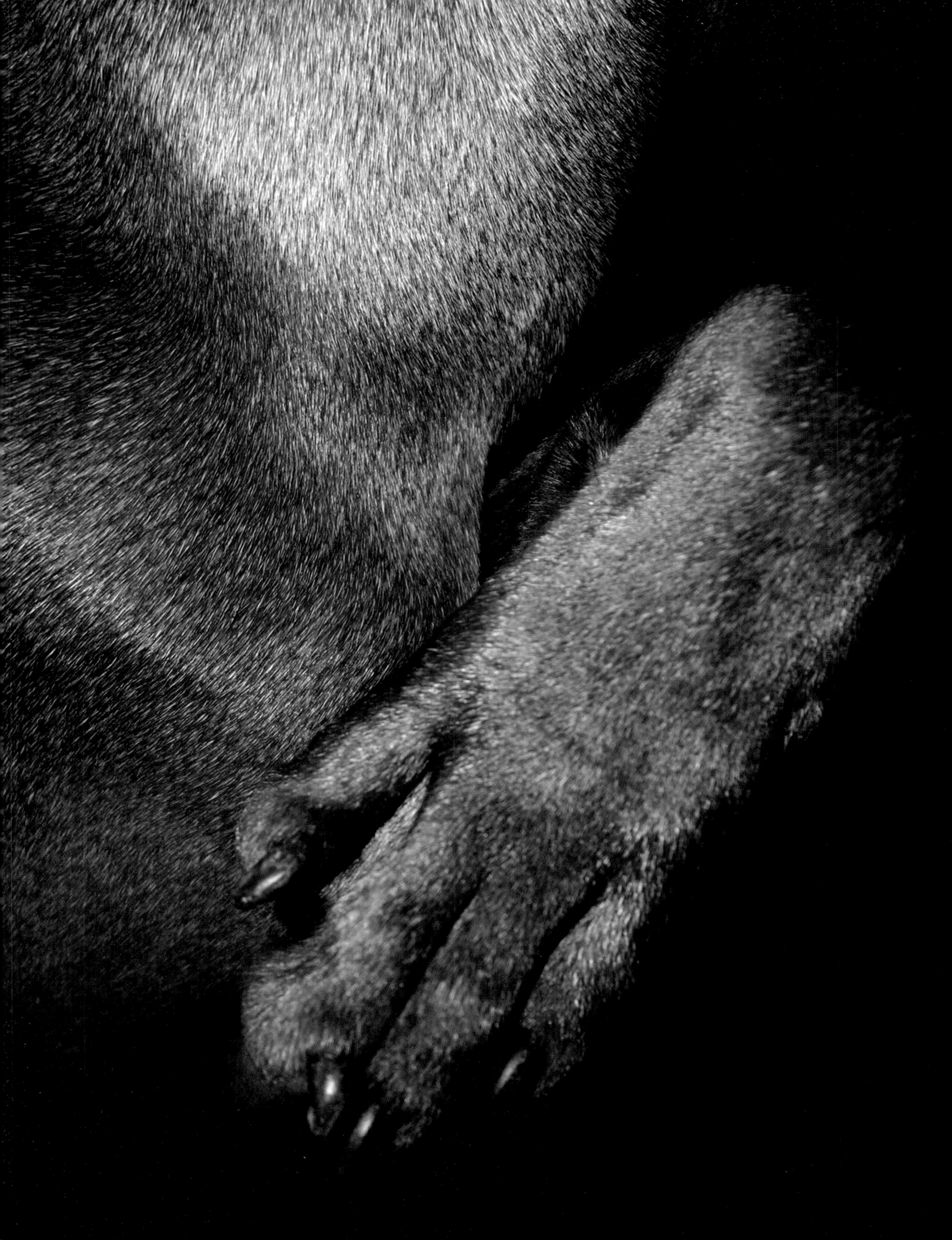

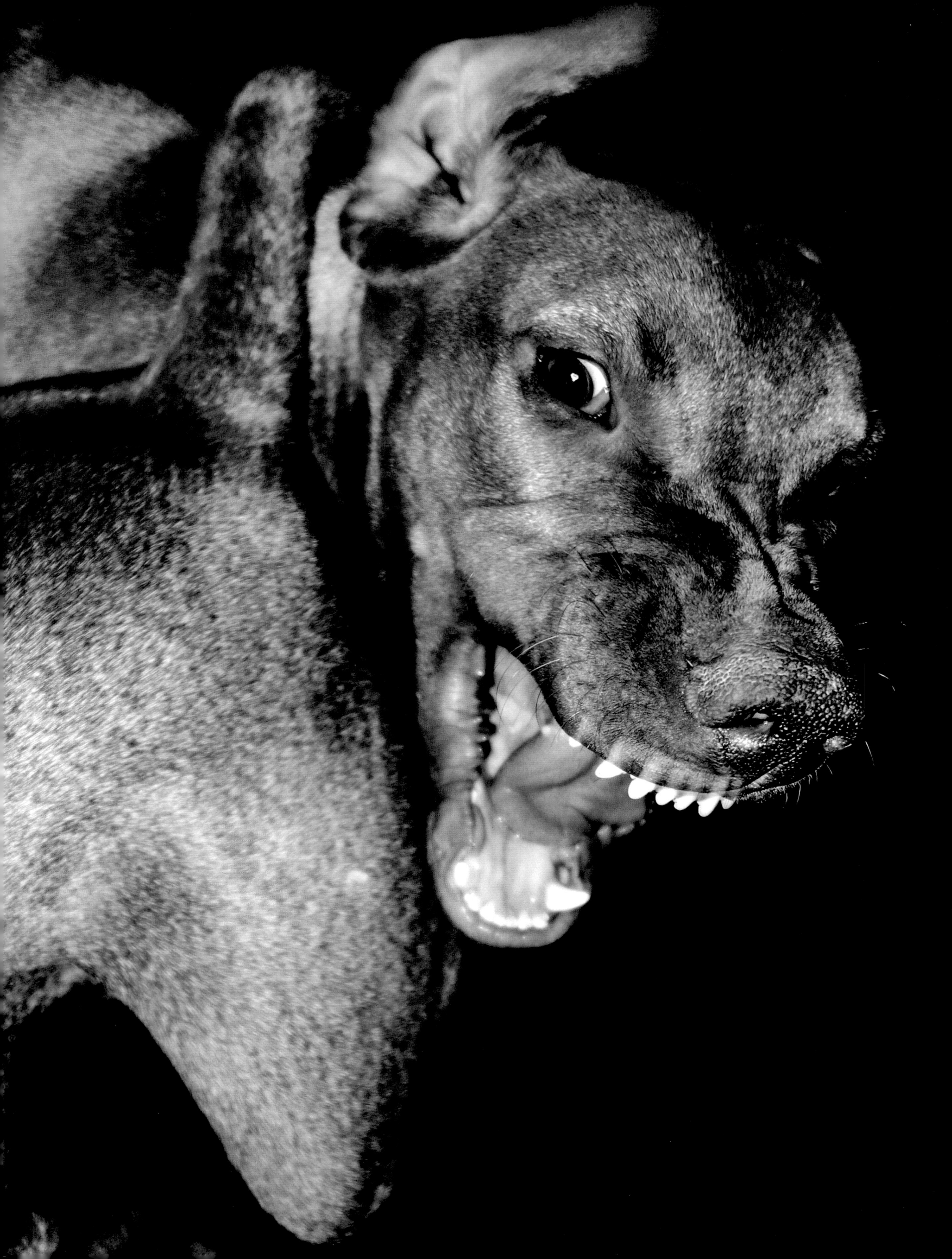

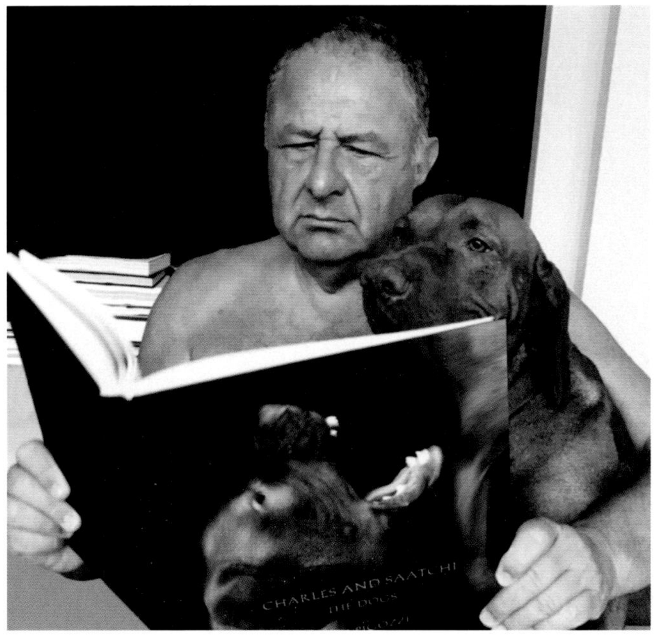

ACKNOWLEDGMENTS

Charles Saatchi, Yolanda Cuomo, Bonnie Briant, Charlotte Phillips,

Annika Murjahn, Zack Chauvin, Pete Valenti